D0363753

Foolproof Cakes

Robinson Publishing Ltd
7 Kensington Church Court
London W8 4SP

First published by Robinson Publishing Ltd 1998
Selection and editorial material © *The Daily Telegraph* 1998
Textual copyright © Various. All rights reserved.

No part of this publication may be reproduced in any form or by any
means without the prior written permission of the publisher.

A copy of the British Library Cataloguing in Publication Data
for this title is available from the British Library.

Every effort has been made by the Publishers and *The Daily Telegraph*
to contact each individual contributor. If any recipe has appeared
without proper acknowledgement, the Publishers and
The Daily Telegraph apologise unreservedly.

ISBN 1 85487 577 9

Editor: Anne Johnson
Designer: Peggy Sadler
Illustrations: © Slatter-Anderson

Printed and bound in the EC

Foolproof
Cakes

VICTORIA COMBE

Robinson
IN COLLABORATION WITH
THE DAILY TELEGRAPH

Contents

Introduction

Fresh back from honeymoon – with sand still in my shoes – my husband John announced that his parents were coming for afternoon tea. I blanched. Tea meant baking cakes – a foreign and mysterious process that I had never dared attempt.

Quivering over my shiny new kitchen scales, I set about making ginger nuts because the recipe claimed they could not fail. But they could – and they did. I had to hide the humiliating brown splodges glued to the baking tray and resort to a box of Mr Kipling.

Knowing that this must not happen again, I appealed for help in a column to readers of *The Daily Telegraph*. Their response was wonderful. I received tried and tested recipes which had been family treasures through the generations, and through both world wars. Given such encouragement, I set about learning how to bake cakes and I am still doing so.

But this book is not about my own misadventures with baking tins. It is founded on the wisdom of readers who were generous enough to impart their own recipes for foolproof cakes which have wooed in-laws, difficult children and even members of the W.I. Inspired by such riches, I felt moved to go back to the mixing bowl.

I began with a Moist Lemon Cake (page 114) from Pam Daniels, of Norwich, which she claimed 'went down a bomb' with the W.I. and had been a favourite of her late husband, who died just before their Golden Wedding Anniversary. Mrs. Daniels insisted on free-range eggs. Admittedly, I was a bit cack-handed at grating the lemon, but coped well with measuring and wielding the food processor. I had to wait 40 minutes for the outcome, but it was worth it. I opened the oven door to see a risen, golden cake. My spirits soared.

I marvelled at the number of women who are so proficient in the art of cake making. In this age of women's emancipation, we are expected to be coy about homely skills. The very idea of a woman in her pinny turning out a perfect cherry cake amounts to incorrect thinking.

Nonetheless, when my cry for help went out, readers rallied with enthusiasm. They seemed to rejoice at the thought that a newly-married woman might worry about the ▉▉▉nts of a cake stand before offering tea to her mother-in-law.

I held a mini-contest on readers' recipes in our Wiltshire kitchen with two little boys who live nearby acting as judges. I made six cakes, all of which claimed to be idiot-proof. They all came off, but Mrs Daniels' Moist Lemon Cake was voted a clear winner by Harry, six, and his three-year-old brother Marcus.

The runners-up also appear in this book. There is a splendid Chocolate Truffle Cake (page 81) from Ann Meddings, of Kingston in Surrey, which works well as a pudding served with crème fraîche and a few summer berries on the side, and a Sticky Ginger Cake (page 5) from Barbara Jackson, of Penicuik in Midlothian.

It was Mrs. Jackson, generously imparting her mother's secret cake recipe, who warned me that home-bakers were a 'very evangelising species'. One mouthful of her Sticky Ginger Cake and my face shone with the look of a new convert.

I have learned, to my astonishment, that I find sweet pleasure from seeing a freshly-baked cake standing proud on a baking tray. I know it is not what is expected of a young woman on a Sunday afternoon, when there is paragliding and deep-sea diving on offer. Yet in a funny sort of way it is exciting and there is plenty of risk. As Adam Lindsay Gordon had it:

> 'There is no game that is worth a rap
> For a rational man to play
> Into which no accident, no mishap
> Can possibly find its way.'

So here I am, the new evangelist. I cannot yet pretend to know all about baking, and I learn more with every cake. But what the authors of these recipes offer is a wealth of knowledge which I hope may inspire other novices like me to dabble in the mixing bowl.

A warning note: there is a lot of kit involved. There

seems no limit to the choice of baking tins. And when it comes to the ingredients, I quake at the variety of flours and sugars on offer. My humble advice is to keep your eye on the kitchen scales. My sister Rachel, who helped to build my confidence in early baking days, advised me that baking was essentially a science. If the chemistry was to work, she said, I needed to be precise in my measurements. Experienced cooks may use a pinch of this and a handful of that. Novices cannot.

Rachel gave me an American Pound Cake recipe (page 25) which she inherited from her great grandmother-in-law from Louisiana. Rachel made this rich, buttery cake for us at home and it was devoured by our three brothers before it had time to cool in the tin. It is a big, hearty cake for hungry chaps.

My mother-in-law, Pam Whitwam, who involuntarily started the whole thing rolling, has considerately passed on her brilliant Chocolate Cake recipe (page 90) which kept her two sons very happy and which husband John chose as a child for his birthday cake. My first attempt won modified praise. Not *quite* as good as Mum made.

Never mind. Novices have to start somewhere. This is meant to be a vote of thanks to so many correspondents who encouraged me to travel down the wiggly road towards perfect cake making.

Thank you.

Victoria Combe

Cake Know-how

Do not be put off by the formidable baking sections in supermarkets, which are always surrounded by brisk, efficient shoppers whom you would never dare ask for advice. Here is a crash course in ingredients which will help you bluff your way to the check-out, unscathed.

Flour

Some people rely on self-raising for every cake, others are fussier about the flours they use.

There are two types: high-gluten (strong) and low-gluten (weak). A strong flour, which is used in bread making, has a gluten content of 10–15 per cent, which gives it good raising power and a light, open texture. A soft flour, with a low gluten of 7–10 per cent, absorbs fat well, gives a smaller rise and a finer texture, and is best for most cakes and biscuits.

Choosing between plain and self-raising is like choosing between an automatic and a geared car. The 'automatic' flour gives you a good balance of raising agents, but with plain flour you can control what you add. The general advice is 2½ teaspoons of baking powder to every 250 g/8 oz plain flour.

Sifting flour makes it easier to mix. Some stalwart bakers swear that sifting flour leads to a lighter cake.

Sugar

Go for caster sugar for sponge cakes, and if you have run out and are desperate, you can always whizz some granulated in a liquidiser/food processor for a similar effect.

Soft brown sugar, dark or light, gives a caramel flavour and is best in ginger cakes and fruit cakes.

Demerara sugar is coarser than granulated and is suitable in cakes where the ingredients are heated before baking so that the sugar dissolves.

Other sweeteners

Treacle gives a lovely dark colour to chocolate, ginger and fruit cakes. It is not as sweet as its blonde sister, golden syrup, which goes well in cakes with spices, such as cinnamon, allspice and nutmeg. Both give a good sticky texture.

Honey is an excellent sweetener, but keep in mind that it is sweeter than sugar. It has a distinctive flavour and also has the great advantage of keeping cakes fresher for longer.

Fat

Most cakes are made with butter or margarine, though some use oil, which is easy to mix but has a rather flat taste. Some people insist that butter tastes better and is worth the extra expense. Do not use butter or margarine straight from the fridge.

Fruit

Dried fruit should be plump and soft. If it has gone horrible and hard, soak it in hot water for a few minutes and drain on kitchen paper.

Eggs

The debate over whether to use free-range or ordinary eggs is complicated and I will not attempt to enter into the right/wrong row over how the chickens are kept. I do know that free-range eggs taste better and have a richer colour, but they cost more.

Be careful when using recipes with raw eggs. The risk of salmonella means that they should not be given to pregnant and nursing mothers, small children or the elderly.

Nuts

Everyone knows the risks of nut allergies and the need to tell people if a cake has any trace of nuts in its ingredients. For some people with an allergy, even touching a walnut on top of a cake could cause a life-threatening reaction. In the light of this, it is advisable not to give cakes containing nuts to very small children without consulting their parents beforehand.

Measurements

Both metric and imperial measurements are given in the recipes. Either is fine, but do not mix the two, as they do vary very slightly.

Standard level spoon measurements are used throughout.
1 tablespoon = 15 ml
1 teaspoon = 5 ml

Preparing the cake tins

First of all, invest in a good variety of tins: two sandwich, one deep tin with a loose bottom, a bun tray, a muffin tray, loaf tins both big and small and a ring tin for special celebration cakes.

Grease the cake tins lightly with softened butter or margarine – preferably unsalted – or you can use oil. Then line the tin with greaseproof paper, which also needs to be thoroughly greased.

For fruit cakes, you need to line the whole tin. You could make the liners yourself if you are a sucker for punishment, or you can buy them in bulk. I use Lakeland Plastics, which have an efficient mail order service.

Sponge cakes need only be lined on the bottom of the tin – ready-cut discs of paper can be bought, or made at home. You will be able to use that school compass again.

With a very rich fruit mixture, which needs a long cooking time, it is a good idea to put a double strip of thick brown paper around the outside of the tin. This helps prevent the outside of the cake overcooking.

Baking cakes

Ovens should always be preheated to the temperature stated in the recipe. If you have a fan-assisted oven, follow the manufacturer's instructions for adjusting times and temperatures. It is usually advisable to shave off five to seven minutes from the time, but no two cookers are exactly the same.

When a cake is cooked, it should be well risen, golden brown, and starting to shrink away from the sides. You can pierce the cake with a skewer and if it comes out clean, with no traces of mixture, the cake is ready.

It can be hard to tell when a cake is cooked. Another way to do this is to press the centre of the top of the cake lighly with a finger. It should feel spongy, give slight resistance to the pressure, and bounce back quickly, leaving no fingermark.

Sponge Cakes

Carrot Cake

250 g/8 oz butter
375 g/12 oz demerara sugar
finely grated rind of 1 orange
4 eggs
300 g/10 oz plain flour
½ teaspoon nutmeg
1 teaspoon cinnamon
1 teaspoon bicarbonate of soda
5–6 medium carrots, grated
175 g/6 oz walnuts, chopped
75 ml/3 fl oz warm water
3 teaspoons baking powder
½ teaspoon salt

1 Grease and line the base of a 23 cm/9 inch round, high-sided cake tin. Preheat the oven to 180°C/350°F/ Gas Mark 4.

2 Cream together the butter, sugar and orange rind. Add the eggs and sift in the flour.

3 Then add the nutmeg, cinnamon, bicarbonate of soda, grated carrots, chopped walnuts, warm water, baking powder and salt. Now give the mixture a really good stir.

4 Put the cake mixture into the prepared cake tin and bake in the preheated oven for 1 hour 10 minutes, or until the top springs back when pressed lightly.

5 Allow the cake to cool in the tin for 5 minutes, then turn out on a cake rack and allow to cool completely.

Tony Hogger
Blackshots, Grays

'Carrot cake's a wonderful thing. You can kid yourself that it's healthier than other cakes and eat several slices without feeling in the least bit guilty.'

Preparation Time	40 minutes
Cooking Time	1 hour 10 minutes
Oven Temperature	180°C/350°F/Gas Mark 4

Reader's Tip

A delicious topping for carrot cake is to mix cream cheese with lemon juice and cover the cake with this.

3

Granny's No-Fail Sponge

3 eggs, separated
75 g/3 oz caster sugar
75 g/3 oz self-raising flour, sifted with ½ teaspoon baking powder
raspberry jam
double cream, whipped with a little caster sugar

1 Grease and flour two 18 cm/7 inch cake tins and preheat the oven to 200°C/400°F/Gas Mark 6.

2 Whisk the egg whites until stiff but not dry. Now add the caster sugar and whisk again to get a glossy finish.

3 Drop in the egg yolks in three different places and whisk for 1 minute.

4 Fold in the sifted flour and baking powder, using a metal spoon.

5 Turn the mixture into the prepared cake tins and bake in the preheated oven for 15 minutes, or until the edges begin to shrink away from the sides. Allow to cool on a cooling rack. Sandwich the two cakes together with raspberry jam and whipped cream.

Emma Gardner
Newtonabbey, Northern Ireland

Preparation Time	15 minutes
Cooking Time	15 minutes
Oven Temperature	200°C/400°F/Gas Mark 6

Reader's Tip

This is a fat-free sponge, which is easier on the tummy – if you don't load on the double cream. When you separate the eggs, try to keep the yolks whole so as to stop any yolk getting into the white.

Sticky Ginger Cake

300 g/10 oz self-raising flour
200 g/7 oz soft light brown sugar
125 g/4 oz butter or margarine
¾ teaspoon bicarbonate of soda
2 teaspoons ginger powder
2 tablespoons golden syrup
1 egg
250 ml/8 fl oz milk

1 Grease and line a 14 x 24 cm/6 x 9½ inch rectangular baking tray, or a 20 cm/8 in square baking tray. Preheat the oven to 180°C/350°F/Gas Mark 4.

2 Put all the ingredients except the milk into a mixing bowl.

3 Heat the milk to boiling point. Pour the hot milk into the bowl, and mix well until really smooth.

4 Pour into the prepared tin and bake in the preheated oven for 30 minutes or until the top springs back when pressed.

5 Leave to cool for 10 minutes before turning out on to a cooling rack.

Barbara Jackson
Penicuik, Midlothian

Preparation Time	10 minutes
Cooking Time	30 minutes
Oven Temperature	180°C/350°F/Gas Mark 4

Reader's Tip

All the ingredients should be at room temperature before use. Do not try to use margarine or butter straight from the fridge

Cherry Layer Cake

150 g/5 oz self-raising flour
125 g/4 oz caster sugar
1 teaspoon baking powder
2 large eggs
7 tablespoons cooking oil
2 tablespoons milk
1 teaspoon vanilla essence
125 g/4 oz glacé cherries, quartered

1 Grease and line two 18 cm/7 inch cake tins or, if you prefer, use 20 little cake cases. Preheat the oven to 200°C/400°F/Gas Mark 6.

2 Sift together the flour, sugar and baking powder.

3 Add the eggs, oil, milk, vanilla essence and glacé cherries. Beat well, using a wooden spoon, or a hand or electric mixer, until all the ingredients are well blended and the mixture is smooth.

4 Divide the mixture between the two prepared cake tins, or the 20 little cake cases. Bake the large cakes for 20 minutes, or the small ones for 10–15 minutes, until the cakes are well risen and springy to the touch.

5 Fill and ice the cakes as you wish.

Gillian and Yvonne
Darlington, County Durham

'This is my mainstay for speed and variety, as the flavourings you use can be varied according to taste. It's honestly impossible to spoil: idiot-proof, and husband-, student daughter- and bachelor brother-proof too.'

Preparation Time	15 minutes
Cooking Time	10–20 minutes
Oven Temperature	200°C/400°F/Gas Mark 6

Reader's Tip

This mixture is much more liquid than the creamed mixture you need for a Victoria sponge — more like a thick batter. If you use individual cake cases, it's a good idea to place these in deep bun tins to help them keep their shape.

Orange Snow Cake

150 g/5 oz margarine
75 g/3 oz caster sugar
2 eggs, separated
250 g/8 oz self-raising flour
2 tablespoons marmalade
rind and juice of 1 orange
icing sugar, for dusting

1 Grease and line the base of an 18 cm/7 inch round, deep-sided cake tin with greaseproof paper. Preheat the oven to 190°C/375°F/Gas Mark 5.

2 Cream together the margarine and sugar, then add the egg yolks. Sift in the flour, and stir in the marmalade, the orange rind and 4 tablespoons of the juice.

3 Whisk the egg whites until stiff. Fold in a couple of tablespoons of egg white, then fold in the rest.

4 Transfer the cake mixture to the prepared tin and bake in the preheated oven for 45 minutes. Check after 30 minutes and if it is browning too much, cover it with greaseproof paper or foil, or move it to a lower shelf. When the cake is cooked, turn out on to a cake rack and allow to cool. Dust the cake with a little icing sugar, for a 'snow' effect.

Tony Hogger
Blackshots, Grays

Preparation Time	20 minutes
Cooking Time	45 minutes
Oven Temperature	190°C/375°F/Gas Mark 5

Reader's Tip

A smooth marmalade is probably your best choice for this cake.

Swiss Roll

125 g/4 oz caster sugar, plus a little extra for dusting
3 eggs
65 g/2½ oz plain flour, sifted
¼ teaspoon salt
warm jam and whipped cream, for filling

1 Preheat the oven to 190°C/375°F/Gas Mark 5. Put the caster sugar on aluminium foil on a heat-resistant plate in the centre of the oven for 6 minutes.

2 Meanwhile, grease a Swiss roll tin and oil a sheet of greaseproof paper cut to the size of the tin.

3 Beat the eggs for 10 minutes and add the sugar. Then gently fold in the flour and salt with a spatula.

4 Spread the mixture evenly into the prepared tin and cook in the preheated oven for 12–15 minutes until golden brown, well risen and springy to the touch.

5 Meanwhile, have ready a sheet of greaseproof paper heavily dusted with caster sugar over a folded newspaper. Run a knife around the edges of the cake, turn it out on to the prepared greaseproof paper. Leave to cool and, after about 30–45 minutes, spread the surface with warmed jam and cream. Roll up with the aid of the paper.

Daphne King-Brewster
Holyhead, North Wales

Preparation Time	30 minutes, plus cooling time
Cooking Time	12–15 minutes
Oven Temperature	190°C/375°F/Gas Mark 5

Reader's Tip

Choose a good-quality jam for the filling, with a high percentage of fruit.

Apple Cake

250 g/8 oz self-raising flour
125 g/4 oz butter or margarine
125 g/4 oz soft light brown sugar
250 g/8 oz peeled and roughly diced cooking apple
1 medium egg
1 tablespoon milk
2 tablespoons caster sugar
$\frac{1}{2}$ teaspoon cinnamon

1 Grease and flour a rectangular baking tin about 28 x 18 cm/11 x 7 inches. Preheat the oven to 200°C/400°F/Gas Mark 6.

2 Sieve the flour into a mixing bowl and rub in the butter or margarine with your fingertips until the mixture resembles fine breadcrumbs.

3 Stir in the brown sugar and cooking apple, then add the egg and the milk to make a fairly stiff mixture, with a reluctant dropping consistency.

4 Mix together the caster sugar and cinnamon, and set aside. Put the cake mixture into the prepared cake tin and sprinkle the reserved mixture of sugar and cinnamon over the top of the cake.

5 Bake in the preheated oven for 30–35 minutes. Turn out and allow to cool on a cake rack, and cut into squares to serve.

Tony Hogger
Blackshots, Grays

'*Bramleys are the best choice of apple for this cake — no question. When they are cooked, they become mouthwateringly fluffy inside.*'

	Makes 16 x 5 cm/2 in squares
Preparation Time	20 minutes
Cooking Time	30–35 minutes
Oven Temperature	200°C/400°F/Gas Mark 6

Reader's Tip

It is best not to slice this cake until it is completely cool, otherwise it has a tendency to fall apart.

11

Buttering Cake

125 g/4 oz margarine.
125 g/4 oz sugar
250 ml/8 fl oz milk
250 g/8 oz dried fruit
250 g/8 oz self-raising flour, sifted
a pinch of salt
¼ teaspoon ground cinnamon (optional)
1 egg, lightly beaten

1 Grease and line a 1 kg/2 lb loaf tin and preheat the oven to 160°C/325°F/Gas Mark 3.

2 Place the margarine, sugar, milk and fruit in a saucepan and heat gently until the sugar is dissolved. Leave to cool for 5 minutes

3 Add the flour, salt and cinnamon, if using. Mix well. Then add the egg and mix everything together with a wooden spoon.

4 Turn out the cake mixture into the prepared loaf tin, then bake in the preheated oven for 1¼ hours. Leave to cool before turning it out, then slice before serving.

Vera Beba
Spalding

Preparation Time	20 minutes
Cooking Time	1¼ hours
Oven Temperature	160°C/325°F/Gas Mark 3

Reader's Tip

Butter the slices of cake before eating them, and enjoy!

Lemon Drizzle Cake

125 g/4 oz hard margarine, softened
75 g/3 oz sugar
2 eggs
150 g/5 oz self-raising flour
2 tablespoons lemon curd
grated rind of ½ large lemon

SYRUP
2 tablespoons granulated sugar
juice of 1 lemon

1 Grease and line a 1 kg/2 lb loaf tin and preheat the oven to 180°C/350°F/Gas Mark 4.

2 Cream together the margarine and sugar until soft. Then add a little of the egg and a little flour alternately. Add the lemon curd and rind.

3 Turn out the cake mixture into the prepared loaf tin and bake for 45 minutes–1 hour.

4 Meanwhile, to make the syrup, heat the sugar gently until dissolved, then add the lemon juice. Take off the heat and allow to cool.

5 When the cake is cooked, take it out of the oven but leave in the tin. Pour over the syrup and leave to cool.

Mrs. N. Ashworth
Lincoln

Preparation Time	20 minutes
Cooking Time	45 minutes–1 hour
Oven Temperature	180°C/350°F/Gas Mark 4

Reader's Tip

If the mixture curdles, add a little more flour while mixing in the egg.

13

Victoria Sponge

175 g/6 oz caster sugar
175 g/6 oz butter at room temperature
3 large eggs at room temperature, beaten
3 drops of vanilla essence
175 g/6 oz self-raising flour, sifted
1½ teaspoons baking powder (optional)
a little milk
caster sugar, for dredging

1 Grease and line two 18 cm/7 inch cake tins and preheat the oven to 190°C/375°F/Gas Mark 5.

2 Cream together the sugar and butter until pale and fluffy. Add the eggs, a little at a time, beating well after each addition, then add the vanilla essence. Fold in half the flour and the baking powder, if using, with a metal spoon, then fold in all the remaining flour and add a few drops of milk to give it a dropping consistency.

3 Place half the mixture in each cake tin and level it with a palette knife. Bake both cakes on the middle shelf of the preheated oven for about 20 minutes, turning the tins halfway through the cooking time, or until well risen, golden brown, firm to the touch and beginning to shrink away from the sides of the tins. Turn out and cool on a wire rack.

4 When the cakes are cool, sandwich them together with cream, jam or butter cream, as you wish, and dredge with caster sugar.

John Wright
Grantown on Spey

'This is the definitive sponge mix, which was passed down from Mr. Wright's grandfather who was a master baker.'

Preparation Time	20 minutes
Cooking Time	about 20 minutes
Oven Temperature	190°C/375°F/Gas Mark 5

Reader's Tip

Do not use eggs straight from the fridge but take them out at least 30 minutes beforehand.

15

Victoria Cake

125 g/4 oz butter, softened
4½ tablespoons caster sugar
2 large eggs
4½ tablespoons self-raising flour, sifted
1 teaspoon water or lemon juice

1 Grease a 15–20 cm/6–8 inch Pyrex casserole dish, which will not stick as easily as a metal cake tin. Preheat the oven to 160°C/325°F/Gas Mark 3.

2 Put the butter in a mixing bowl and then rub in the sugar using your fingers.

3 Break in 1 of the eggs and mix in. Spoon in 1 table-spoon flour and mix in, then add the other egg and another tablespoon flour. Mix in the water or lemon juice, then tip in the remaining flour and mix this in, too.

4 Transfer the cake mixture to the prepared casserole dish and bake in the preheated oven for 1¼ hours. Then turn off the oven and leave the cake in the oven for another 15 minutes.

5 Allow the cake to cool, then run a knife blade around the dish and invert the cake.

Vera Hopwood
Craven Arms, Shropshire

Preparation Time	20 minutes
Cooking Time	1¼ hours
Oven Temperature	160°C/325°F/Gas Mark 3

Reader's Tip

A good way of softening the butter is to slice it and leave it in a plastic mixing bowl for a couple of hours at (warm) room temperature.

Yogurt Cake

250 g/8 oz self-raising flour
125 g/4 oz sugar
1 egg
a few drops vanilla essence
50 ml/2 fl oz oil
125 g/4 oz plain yogurt

1 Grease and line a 1 kg/2 lb loaf tin and preheat the oven to 180°C/350°F/Gas Mark 4.

2 Combine the flour with the sugar, then beat in the egg, vanilla essence, oil and yogurt.

3 Pour the cake mixture into the prepared loaf tin and bake in the preheated oven for 1 hour. Turn out on to a cooling rack.

M. Atkinson
Wetherby

Preparation Time	10 minutes
Cooking Time	1 hour
Oven Temperature	180°C/350°F/Gas Mark 4

Reader's Tip

This yogurt cake is especially good when it is spread with a little of your favourite jam.

17

Cinnamon Cake

250 g/8 oz plain flour
2 teaspoons baking powder
a pinch of salt
1 teaspoon cinnamon
125 g/4 oz butter or margarine
175 g/6 oz caster sugar
2 eggs, separated
150 ml/¼ pint milk

TOPPING
1 tablespoon melted butter
½ teaspoon cinnamon
50 g/2 oz caster sugar
25 g/1 oz cornflakes

1 Grease a 23 cm/9 inch cake tin. Preheat the oven to 190°C/375°F/Gas Mark 5.

2 Sift together the flour, baking powder, salt and cinnamon into a large mixing bowl.

3 Add the butter or margarine, sugar and egg yolks, and mix together well.

4 Add the milk and stir until combined.

5 Beat the egg whites until stiff and then fold into the cake mixture.

6 Transfer the mixture to the prepared cake tin.

7 To make the topping, melt the butter and stir in the cinnamon, sugar and cornflakes. Scatter over the top of the cake.

8 Bake for about 30–35 minutes until cooked.

Moira Bourke
Glasgow

> *'It was an inspired idea to use cornflakes in the topping — they give a deliciously crunchy texture.'*

Preparation Time	25 minutes
Cooking Time	30–35 minutes
Oven Temperature	190°C/375°F/Gas Mark 5

Reader's Tip

Use either the 'old-fashioned' (imperial) measures or the new (metric) ones as you prefer, but never mix the two.

19

Wartime Gingerbread

250 g/8 oz sugar
250 ml/8 fl oz water
175 g/6 oz dried fruit
2 tablespoons black treacle
75 g/3 oz margarine
a few pieces of ginger in syrup, chopped, plus a little of the syrup
50 g/2 oz almonds, chopped
150 g/5 oz flour, sifted
1 teaspoon cinnamon
1 teaspoon ginger
1 teaspoon allspice
1 teaspoon baking powder
½ teaspoon bicarbonate of soda

1 Grease and line a 1 kg/2 lb loaf tin. Preheat the oven to 180°C/350°F/Gas Mark 4.

2 Put the sugar, water, dried fruit, black treacle, margarine, ginger, syrup and chopped almonds in a saucepan, and bring to the boil. Boil for 3 minutes, then allow to cool. When the mixture is cold, stir and add the flour, cinnamon, ginger, allspice, baking powder and bicarbonate of soda dissolved in a little hot water. Mix well.

3 Transfer the cake mixture to the prepared loaf tin and bake in the preheated oven for 1 hour.

Sarah Innes
Colinsburgh Leven, Fife

Preparation Time	20 minutes, plus cooling time
Cooking Time	1 hour
Oven Temperature	180°C/350°F/Gas Mark 4

😊 *Reader's Tip*

This was given to me by my 90-year-old sister-in-law. It has no eggs, which were rationed during the war.

Seed Cake

175 g/6 oz soft margarine
175 g/6 oz caster sugar
3 medium eggs
250 g/8 oz self-raising flour
1 teaspoon caraway seeds

1 Grease and line an 18 cm/7 inch cake tin. Preheat the oven to 160°C/325°F/Gas Mark 3.

2 Place all the ingredients in a mixing bowl and mix together well. Place the cake mixture in the prepared cake tin and bake on the middle shelf of the preheated oven for 1½ hours.

3 When the cake is cooked, turn out on to a cooling rack and allow to cool.

Ivy Jarvis
Framfield, Sussex

'Ivy is an old pal of my grandfather's and, after much coaxing, she parted with this no-fail cake.'

Preparation Time	10 minutes
Cooking Time	1½ hours
Oven Temperature	160°C/325°F/Gas Mark 3

Reader's Tip

Caraway seeds, which have a distinctive flavour, are a favourite ingredient in central and northern Europe.

All-in-One Sponge

175 g/6 oz self-raising flour, sifted
1 teaspoon baking powder
175 g/6 oz soft margarine
175 g/6 oz caster sugar
2 large eggs
2–3 drops vanilla essence

1 Grease and line two 18 cm/7 inch cake tins, no less than 2.5 cm/1 inch deep. Preheat the oven to 160°C/325°F/Gas Mark 3.

2 Combine all the ingredients in a mixing bowl and whisk with an electric hand whisk for 1 minute, or until everything is thoroughly mixed.

3 Divide the mixture between the two prepared cake tins, level off the cake mixture with a knife and bake on the centre shelf of the preheated oven for about 35 minutes, or until the cakes are coming away from the sides of the tins and the centre springs back when gently pressed with a finger.

4 When the cakes are cooked, leave them in the tins for about 30 seconds before turning them out on to a cake rack to cool.

5 When the cakes are cool, sandwich them together with jam or sliced strawberries and whipped cream.

Jill M. White
Tavistock, Devon

'This is quick and easy to make and looks most impressive at a summer tea party.'

Preparation Time	10 minutes
Cooking Time	35 minutes
Oven Temperature	160°C/325°F/Gas Mark 3

Reader's Tip

This cake is easy to adapt into a chocolate cake by omitting the vanilla and adding 2 tablespoons of sifted cocoa and 1 tablespoon of milk. When the cakes are cool, sandwich them together with 150 g/ 5 oz of good-quality plain chocolate mixed with 150 ml/5 fl oz of soured cream. Decorate the top of the cake with the same mixture.

Banana Bread

125 g/4 oz butter
150 g/5 oz caster sugar
2 large eggs
3 bananas
75 g/3 oz walnuts, coarsely chopped
250 g/8 oz self-raising flour, sifted
½ teaspoon salt

1 Line a 23 cm/9 inch loaf tin with greaseproof paper. Brush with melted butter and set aside. Preheat the oven to 180°C/350°F/Gas Mark 4.

2 Cream together the butter and sugar until fluffy, then beat in the eggs.

3 Peel and mash the bananas with a fork and add them to the mixture, together with the walnuts. Fold in the flour and salt.

4 Spoon the mixture into the prepared loaf tin and bake in the preheated oven for 1 hour.

5 When the cake is cooked, turn it out on a wire rack and allow to cool.

Moira Bourke
Glasgow

Preparation Time	25 minutes
Cooking Time	1 hour
Oven Temperature	180°C/350°F/Gas Mark 4

Reader's Tip

If you have a fan-assisted oven, you should reduce the cooking time by about 5–7 minutes.

American Pound Cake

375 g/12 oz butter
250 g/8 oz cream cheese
700 g/23 oz sugar
a pinch of salt
1½ teaspoons vanilla essence
6 eggs
375 g/12 oz plain flour, sifted

1 Grease a ring cake tin and preheat the oven to 160°C/325°F/Gas Mark 3.

2 Put the butter and cream cheese in a food processor and mix until pale and creamy.

3 Add the sugar, salt and vanilla essence, and mix until very pale and creamy.

4 Add the eggs 1 at a time, mixing thoroughly after each addition. Pour into a large mixing bowl, and fold in the flour.

5 Bake in the prepared ring cake tin in the preheated oven for 1–1½ hours.

Rachel Perry
East Molesey, Surrey

Preparation Time	15 minutes
Cooking Time	1–1½ hours
Oven Temperature	160°C/325°F/Gas Mark 3

Reader's Tip

To test that the cake is cooked, insert a skewer. If it comes out clean, the cake is done.

Orange Cake

125 g/4 oz soft margarine
125 g/4 oz caster sugar
75 g/3 oz self-raising flour, sifted
2 eggs, beaten
4 tablespoons milk
grated rind of 1 orange

ORANGE SYRUP
juice of 1 orange
50 g/2 oz caster sugar

1 Grease and line an 18 cm/7 inch cake tin. Preheat the oven to 180°C/350°F/Gas Mark 4.

2 Cream together the margarine and sugar in a mixing bowl. Gradually mix in the flour, eggs, milk and orange rind until you have a fairly smooth mixture.

3 Put the cake mixture in the prepared cake tin and bake in the preheated oven for about 30 minutes, until the cake is coming away from the sides of the tin and the centre springs back when gently pressed with a finger.

4 Meanwhile, make the orange syrup. Heat the orange juice and caster sugar in a saucepan over a low heat until the sugar is dissolved.

5   When the cake is cooked, leave it in the tin and prick
    over the surface with the prongs of a fork or a knitting
needle. Pour the syrup carefully over the cake and leave
until quite cold.

Mrs. J.T. Kenner
Taunton, Somerset

'This is a lovely alternative to lemon cake — still with a strong citrus flavour but not quite so tangy.'

Preparation Time	20 minutes
Cooking Time	about 30 minutes
Oven Temperature	180°C/350°F/Gas Mark 4

Reader's Tip

Check whether the cake is cooked after 25 minutes in case your oven cooks more quickly — ovens vary a lot. If it is not ready, return the cake to the oven and cook for another 5 minutes or so.

Banana and Honey Teabread

125 g/4 oz butter or margarine
50 g/2 oz soft brown sugar
2 tablespoons clear honey
2 eggs, beaten
175 g/6 oz self-raising flour
2 large ripe bananas
1 teaspoon ground mixed spice

1 Grease and line a 1 kg/2 lb loaf tin with greaseproof paper, then grease the paper. Preheat the oven to 180°C/350°F/Gas Mark 4.

2 Cream together the butter or margarine, sugar and honey, until the mixture is light and fluffy.

3 Beat in the eggs, a little at a time, adding 1 tablespoon of flour after each addition of egg.

4 Peel and mash the bananas. Stir the mashed bananas into the creamed mixture. Sift together the remaining flour and mixed spice, and fold carefully into the creamed mixture until evenly incorporated.

5 Pour into the prepared loaf tin, level the surface and bake in the preheated oven for 1¼–1½ hours until firm to the touch.

6 Leave to cool in the tin for 1 minute, then turn out on to a wire rack and carefully peel off the lining paper. Turn the cake right way up, and leave to cool completely. Serve sliced, spread with butter if liked.

Gloria Cann
White Waltham, Berkshire

'This teabread is an ideal way of using up over-ripe, discoloured bananas. It's also delicious.'

Preparation Time	25 minutes
Cooking Time	1¼–1½ hours
Oven Temperature	180°C/350°F/Gas Mark 4

Reader's Tip

The cooked teabread freezes particularly well. Simply wrap it up in a polythene bag, seal, label and freeze for up to 2 months. To thaw, unwrap the teabread and leave it to stand at room temperature for 4 hours. It will keep beautifully moist and fresh for up to 4 or 5 days after thawing.

Easy Apple Cake

500 g/1 lb cooking apples
175 g/6 oz self-raising flour, sifted
1 teaspoon baking powder
175 g/6 oz caster sugar
2 eggs
½ teaspoon almond essence
125 g/4 oz butter, melted
caster sugar, to sprinkle

1 Line a 20 cm/8 inch loose-bottom cake tin with greaseproof paper. Heat the oven to 180°C/350°F/Gas Mark 4.

2 Peel, core and finely slice the apples and put them in a bowl of water.

3 Put the flour and baking powder in a bowl with the caster sugar.

4 Beat together the eggs and almond essence, and stir into the flour together with the melted butter. Mix together well.

5 Spread half the mixture into the prepared cake tin.

6 Drain and dry the apples on kitchen paper, and arrange on top of the cake mixture.

7 Top with the remaining cake mixture.

8 Bake the cake in the preheated oven for $1\frac{1}{4}$ hours, or until the cake is golden brown. Then leave to cool for 15 minutes.

Ann Meddings
Kingston, Surrey

'I first tasted this yummy cake when I was a schoolgirl — now, at last, I have the recipe.'

Preparation Time	15 minutes
Cooking Time	$1\frac{1}{4}$ hours
Oven Temperature	180°C/350°F/Gas Mark 4

Reader's Tip

You can buy a useful gadget that both cores and slices an apple in one operation from most good kitchen shops.

Fruit
Cakes

Date Cake

250 ml/8 fl oz boiling water
125–175 g/4–6 oz dates
50 g/2 oz butter
125 g/4 oz caster sugar
1 egg
250 g/8 oz self-raising flour, sifted
1 teaspoon bicarbonate of soda

1 Grease and line the base of a 1.2 litre/2 pint loaf tin and preheat the oven to 180°C/350°F/Gas Mark 4.

2 Pour the boiling water over the dates in a bowl and leave for 20 minutes.

3 Cream together the butter and sugar in a mixing bowl. Add the egg, flour and bicarbonate of soda to the dates (including the liquid), then add this mixture to the creamed butter and sugar.

4 Place the mixture in the prepared loaf tin and bake in the preheated oven for about 1 hour until golden and firm to the touch. Turn out and cool on a wire rack.

E. Ridout
New Malden, Essex

Preparation Time	15 minutes, plus 20 minutes soaking time
Cooking Time	1 hour
Oven Temperature	180°C/350°F/Gas Mark 4

Reader's Tip

Soaking the dates in boiling water softens them and keeps them moist.

Fruit Teabread

300 g/10 oz sultanas and raisins, mixed
200 g/7 oz soft brown sugar
300 ml/½ pint cold tea, strained
1 large egg
300 g/10 oz wholewheat flour

1 Grease and line a 1 kg/2 lb loaf tin, making sure that the lining paper is sufficiently high at the ends to enable you to take the cake out of the tin easily when it is cooked. Preheat the oven to 160°C/325°F/Gas Mark 3.

2 Put the fruit and sugar in a large mixing bowl. Pour over the cold tea and leave overnight.

3 The following day, stir the mixture, add the egg and flour, and mix until smooth. Pour into the prepared tin and level the top of the mixture. Bake in the centre of the preheated oven for 1¼–1½ hours until a sharp skewer comes out clean.

Mrs M. West

Preparation Time	10 minutes, plus overnight soaking time
Cooking Time	1¼–1½ hours
Oven Temperature	160°C/325°F/Gas Mark 3

Reader's Tip

Choose your favourite variety of tea to make this cake. If you like Earl Grey, for example, use that to soak the fruit and sugar.

All-in-One Fruit Cake

250 g/8 oz self-raising flour
1 teaspoon mixed spice
125 g/4 oz soft margarine
2 eggs
125 ml/4 fl oz milk
125 g/4 oz caster sugar
375/12 oz mixed dried fruit

1 Grease and line a 1 kg/2 lb loaf tin and preheat the oven to 160°C/325°F/Gas Mark 3.

2 Sift the flour and mixed spice together. Add all the remaining ingredients and beat them together for 2–3 minutes until thoroughly mixed.

3 Place the cake mixture in the prepared loaf tin and bake in the centre of the preheated oven for about 1¾ hours. Test with a knife – if it comes out clean, it is ready.

4 Allow the cake to cool in the tin for 10 minutes and then transfer to a cooling rack to cool completely.

Liz Kirkwood
Pettswood, Kent

Preparation Time	15 minutes
Cooking Time	1¾ hours
Oven Temperature	160°C/325°F/Gas Mark 3

Reader's Tip

This recipe leaves plenty of scope for variation. You can use any dried fruits that you like: sultanas, currants, raisins, glacé cherries, or any other dried fruits that take your fancy. You can also add almond or vanilla essence to the milk, as you prefer.

Date and Ginger Slab

125 g/4 oz butter
125 g/4 oz soft brown sugar
50 g/2 oz golden syrup
50–75 g/2–3 oz chopped dates
2 large or 3 small eggs, beaten
175 g/6 oz self-raising flour, sifted
2 teaspoons ginger
2 teaspoons bicarbonate of soda

1 Grease and line two 1 kg/2 lb loaf tins and preheat the oven to 160°C/325°F/Gas Mark 3.

2 Melt the butter with the sugar, syrup and dates in a large saucepan. Leave to cool a little. Then add the eggs, flour, ginger and bicarbonate of soda, and mix well.

3 Put the cake mixture in the prepared loaf tins and cook in the preheated oven for about 1–1¼ hours until cooked.

Mrs N. Ashworth
Lincoln

'The first time I made this cake, it sunk because I opened the door too often – a warning.'

Preparation Time	15 minutes
Cooking Time	1–1¼ hours
Oven Temperature	160°C/325°F/Gas Mark 3

Reader's Tip

This cake freezes well once it is cooked. Spread with butter to serve.

Cut and Come Again Cake

250 g/8 oz self-raising flour, sifted
¼ teaspoon salt
1 teaspoon mixed spice
125 g/4 oz sugar
275 g/9 oz mixed dried fruit
1 teaspoon grated orange or lemon rind
125 g/4 oz soft margarine
150 ml/¼ pint milk and water mixed
1 egg, beaten

1 Grease and line a 15 cm/6 inch cake tin or a 1 kg/2 lb loaf tin, and preheat the oven to 180°C/350°F/Gas Mark 4.

2 Mix together all the dry ingredients, then add the margarine, milk and water and the beaten egg. Turn out the mixture into the prepared cake or loaf tin.

3 Bake in the preheated oven for 1 hour 15–20 minutes until well risen, golden brown, firm to the touch and beginning to shrink away from the sides of the tin.

Jenny Heughan
Theydon Bois, Essex

Preparation Time	10 minutes
Cooking Time	1 hour 15–20 minutes
Oven Temperature	180°C/350°F/Gas Mark 4

Reader's Tip

The sugar in this recipe may be brown or white, as you prefer.

Bara Brith

1 mug hot tea
1 mug brown sugar
1 mug mixed dried fruit
2 mugs self-raising flour, sifted
1 egg

1 Butter and line an oblong 500 g/1 lb cake tin and pre-heat the oven to 180°C/350°F/Gas Mark 4.

2 Put the hot tea in a bowl, then add the sugar and dried fruit. Stir well to dissolve the sugar and leave to stand overnight.

3 The following day, add the flour and egg. Beat well and turn into the prepared cake tin. Bake in the pre-heated oven for 45–50 minutes, or until a skewer inserted into the centre of the cake comes out clean.

4 Turn out on to a cooling rack and allow to cool.

Barbara Steele
Swansea, Wales

Preparation Time	15 minutes, plus overnight standing time
Cooking Time	45–50 minutes
Oven Temperature	180°C/350°F/Gas Mark 4

Reader's Tip

Cut this cake into thin slices and butter. Just delicious!

Marmalade Fruit Cake

125 g/4 oz soft margarine
125 g/4 oz soft light brown sugar
375 g/12 oz mixed fruit
1 tablespoon marmalade
250 ml/8 fl oz warm water
250 g/8 oz self-raising flour
½ teaspoon bicarbonate of soda
1 teaspoon mixed spice
2 eggs, lightly beaten

1 Lightly grease and line a 20 cm/8 inch cake tin and preheat the oven to 160°C/325°F/Gas Mark 3.

2 Place the soft margarine, soft brown sugar, mixed fruit, marmalade and warm water in a saucepan and bring gently to a simmer over low heat. Simmer for just 3 minutes, then allow to cool.

3 Sift together all the remaining dry ingredients, including the self-raising flour, the bicarbonate of soda and the mixed spice, into a large mixing bowl.

4 Now add the cooled fruit mixture to the flour, then add the eggs and mix together thoroughly.

5 Pour the cake mixture into the prepared cake tin and bake in the preheated oven for about 1 hour–1 hour 10 minutes.

6 Leave in the tin to cool, then turn out on to a wire rack and leave until completely cold.

Gwen Stevenson
Haywards Heath, East Sussex

'If you're fond of marmalade, you'll just love this cake. I find home-made marmalade tastes better.'

Preparation Time	20 minutes, plus cooling time
Cooking Time	1 hour–1 hour 10 minutes
Oven Temperature	160°C/325°F/Gas Mark 3

Reader's Tip

The marmalade adds something special to this cake. Use orange, lemon or lime marmalade – even ginger marmalade – as you wish. You can, of course, omit it completely if you don't like marmalade, though you'll also have to change the name of the cake.

41

Tea Loaf

375 g/12 oz dried mixed fruit
175 g/6 oz soft brown sugar
a little tea (enough to cover the fruit)
300 g/10 oz self-raising flour
1 teaspoon mixed spice
1 teaspoon cinnamon
1 egg, beaten

1 Soak the dried fruit and sugar overnight in the tea.

2 The following day, stir in the flour, mixed spice, cinnamon and beaten egg.

3 Grease and line two 500 g/1 lb loaf tins and preheat the oven to 180°C/350°F/Gas Mark 4.

4 Divide the mixture into the two prepared loaf tins and bake in the preheated oven for about 45 minutes. Turn out on to a cooling rack and cool.

5 Slice and eat, with or without butter, as preferred.

Norah Hinde
Redcar, Cleveland

Preparation Time	15 minutes, plus overnight soaking time
Cooking Time	45 minutes
Oven Temperature	180°C/350°F/Gas Mark 4

Reader's Tip

The beauty of this cake recipe – quite apart from the fact that it is absolutely delicious – is that it is totally fat free.

Light Fruit Cake

150 g/5 oz butter or margarine
125 g/4 oz caster sugar
3 eggs
250 g/8 oz self-raising flour
250 g/8 oz currants
250 g/8 oz raisins
125 g/4 oz cherries
75 g/3 oz ground almonds
1 tablespoon milk

1 Grease and line a 20 cm/8 inch round cake tin. Preheat the oven to 160°C/325°F/Gas Mark 3.

2 Cream together the butter or margarine and sugar, then add the eggs, flour, fruit, almonds and milk, and mix well.

3 Turn out the cake mixture into the prepared cake tin and bake in the preheated oven for about 2 hours or until the cake springs back when pressed in the centre.

Mrs J.V. Moss
Whitehaven, Cumbria

Preparation Time	20 minutes
Cooking Time	2 hours
Oven Temperature	160°C/325°F/Gas Mark 3

 Reader's Tip

This cake takes very little time to prepare and a long time to cook. It is well worth it.

Farmhouse Fruit Cake

125 g/4 oz plain flour
a pinch of salt
125 g/4 oz wholewheat flour
2 teaspoons baking powder
1 teaspoon mixed spice
$\frac{1}{2}$ teaspoon ground cinnamon
125 g/4 oz soft brown sugar
125 g/4 oz butter or margarine
250 g/8 oz mixed dried fruit
50 g/2 oz chopped mixed peel
3 eggs, beaten
2 tablespoons marmalade
2 tablespoons milk (optional)

1 Grease and line a 20 cm/8 inch round cake tin with greased greaseproof paper. Preheat the oven to 160°C/325°F/Gas Mark 3.

2 Sift the flour and salt into a mixing bowl, then stir in the wholewheat flour, baking powder, mixed spice, cinnamon and sugar.

3 Rub in the butter or margarine. Stir in the remaining ingredients and mix well. Stir in a little milk if the mixture seems too stiff. The cake mixture should be of a reluctant dropping consistency.

4 Spoon into the prepared cake tin and bake in the pre-heated oven for about 1– 1¼ hours or until a skewer inserted in the centre comes out clean. Cover the top of the cake with greaseproof paper if the cake begins to become too brown during the cooking.

5   Remove from the oven, take out of the tin and discard the greaseproof paper. Cool on a wire rack and store in an airtight tin.

Diane Lawton
Marlow Bottom, Buckinghamshire

'This is a deliciously wholesome fruit cake.'

Preparation Time	15 minutes
Cooking Time	1–1¼ hours
Oven Temperature	160°C/325°F/Gas Mark 3

Reader's Tip

Farmhouse fruit cake is a country recipe using wholewheat flour, which is – as you know – much better for you. It keeps well and even improves with age – if given the chance.

Fruity Gingerbread

125 g/4 oz butter
125 g/4 oz soft brown sugar
125 g/4 oz black treacle
1 egg, beaten
125 g/4 oz plain flour
2 teaspoons ground ginger
2 teaspoons ground cinnamon
125 g/4 oz wholewheat flour
about 150 ml/¼ pint warm milk
1 teaspoon bicarbonate of soda
50 g/2 oz mixed dried fruit

1 Grease and line a rectangular 23 x 15 cm/9 x 6 inch cake tin or a 20 cm/8 inch round cake tin with grease-proof paper. Preheat the oven to 150°C/300°F/Gas Mark 2.

2 Put the butter, sugar and treacle in a saucepan and heat gently over low heat until melted, stirring constantly. Allow to cool slightly, then beat in the egg.

3 Sift the plain flour and spices into a mixing bowl, then stir in the wholewheat flour and melted butter mixture, and beat well to combine.

4 Mix the milk with the bicarbonate of soda and add this to the mixture in the bowl. Stir in the fruit. The mixture should have a soft dropping consistency. If the mixture seems too dry, add a little more milk.

5 Spoon the mixture into the prepared cake tin. Bake in the preheated oven for about 1 hour 10 minutes, or until a skewer inserted in the centre comes out clean.

6 Leave the cake to cool in the tin, then remove the cake from the tin and discard the greaseproof paper.

Diane Lawton
Marlow Bottom, Buckinghamshire

'*Prunes and dried apricots can be used instead of dates in this recipe.*'

Preparation Time	25 minutes
Cooking Time	1 hour 10 minutes
Oven Temperature	150°C/300°F/Gas Mark 2

Reader's Tip

Gingerbread always improves and becomes moist and soft if it is kept for a while before eating. When it is cold, place it in an airtight tin and leave for about a week. Then cut into squares.

Date and Walnut Loaf

250 g/8 oz stoned dates, chopped
1 teaspoon bicarbonate of soda
a pinch of salt
300 ml/½ pint hot water
300 g/10 oz self-raising flour
125 g/4 oz butter or margarine, cut in pieces
50 g/2 oz shelled walnuts, chopped
125 g/4 oz dark soft brown sugar
1 egg, beaten

1   Grease a 1 kg/2 lb loaf tin. Preheat the oven to 180°C/350°F/Gas Mark 4.

2   Put the dates, bicarbonate of soda and salt in a mixing bowl and pour over the hot water. Set aside until cool.

3   Meanwhile, sift the flour into a mixing bowl. Add the butter or margarine and rub into the flour. Stir in the walnuts and sugar until thoroughly combined.

4   Mix the dry ingredients into the cooled date mixture and beat in the egg. Pour into the prepared loaf tin and bake in the preheated oven for 1–1¼ hours or until a skewer inserted in the centre comes out clean. Turn out on to a wire cooling rack and leave to cool.

Diane Lawton
Marlow Bottom, Buckinghamshire

Preparation Time	15 minutes, plus cooling time
Cooking Time	1–1¼ hours
Oven Temperature	180°C/350°F/Gas Mark 4

🧁 *Reader's Tip*

This makes the perfect teatime treat. It actually improves with age as long as it is kept in an airtight tin.

Vinegar Fruit Cake

175 g/6 oz butter or margarine
375 g/12 oz self-raising flour
175 g/6 oz sugar
250 g/8 oz sultanas
1 teaspoon mixed spice (optional)
1 teaspoon bicarbonate of soda
2 tablespoons vinegar
300 ml/½ pint milk

1 Grease and flour a 20 cm/8 inch cake tin. Preheat the oven to 190°C/375°F/Gas Mark 5.

2 Mix together the fat and flour, then add the sugar, sultanas and mixed spice, if using.

3 Stir the bicarbonate of soda and vinegar into the milk and add this mixture to all the other ingredients.

4 Pour the cake mixture into the prepared cake tin. Bake in the preheated oven for about 1½ hours, or until a skewer or metal knitting needle inserted into the centre of the cake comes out clean.

Rosemary Cowan
Penzance, Cornwall

Preparation Time	15 minutes, plus overnight soaking
Cooking Time	1½ hours
Oven Temperature	190°C/375°F/Gas Mark 5

Reader's Tip

Vinegar might seem like a strange addition, but fear not – it's actually remarkably good.

Cider Cake

375 g/12 oz mixed dried fruit
175 g/6 oz soft dark sugar
300 ml/¹/₂ pint medium sweet cider
1 large egg, beaten
50 g/2 oz butter, melted
375 g/12 oz self-raising flour, sifted

1　Grease and line a 1 kg/2 lb loaf tin with baking parchment. Preheat the oven to 190°C/375°F/Gas Mark 5.

2　Soak the dried fruit and sugar in the cider overnight.

3　The following day, add the beaten egg and melted butter to the fruit mixture. Fold in the flour. At this stage, the mixture should be quite soft.

4　Spoon the mixture into the prepared loaf tin and bake in the preheated oven for 1 hour–1 hour 20 minutes. Test with a wooden skewer after 1 hour, and if the skewer is clean on withdrawal, the cake is cooked.

5　Cool the cake on a cake rack. This cake is best after a couple of days' storage in a cake tin with a well-fitting lid. Do not use a plastic cake box. It freezes well, too. Serve sliced, plain or spread with butter.

Jill M. White
Tavistock, Devon

Preparation Time	15 minutes, plus overnight soaking
Cooking Time	1 hour–1 hour 20 minutes
Oven Temperature	190°C/375°F/Gas Mark 5

Reader's Tip

If this cake is browning too much during the cooking process, cover it with aluminium foil.

Mincemeat Fruit Cake

250 g/8 oz self-raising flour
3 eggs
500 g/1 lb mincemeat
150 g/5 oz caster sugar or soft brown sugar
150 g/5 oz soft margarine
75 g/3 oz sultanas
25 g/1 oz flaked almonds (optional)

1 Grease and line a 20 cm/8 inch cake tin with grease-proof paper, and grease again. Preheat the oven to 160°C/ 325°F/Gas Mark 3.

2 Place all the ingredients, except the almonds, in a bowl and beat together well for about 1 minute.

3 Put the cake mixture into the tin, sprinkle the flaked almonds on the top, if liked, and bake in the pre-heated oven for 1¾ hours. When the cake is cooked, the sides will shrink away from the tin and a skewer put into the middle of the cake should come out clean. Leave the cake in the tin for a few minutes and then allow to cool completely on a cake rack.

Phillip D. Pearson
Kingswinford, West Midlands

Preparation Time	10 minutes
Cooking Time	1¾ hours
Oven Temperature	160°C/325°F/Gas Mark 3

 *Reader's Tip*

If any children are likely to be eating this cake, do not use the almonds in case of nut allergies.

Boiled Fruit Cake

250 g/8 oz mixed dried fruit
a few chopped glacé cherries
125 g/4 oz margarine
175 g/6 oz self-raising flour
1 teaspoon mixed spice
175 g/6 oz sugar
2 eggs, beaten
a little demerara sugar, for sprinkling

1 Grease and line a 1 kg/2 lb loaf tin. Preheat the oven to 180°C/350°F/Gas Mark 4.

2 Put the fruit into a saucepan, cover with water and boil for 5 minutes, then remove from the heat. Drain off the water and add all the remaining ingredients, except for the demerara sugar, to the pan and mix well.

3 Pour the cake mixture into the prepared loaf tin. Sprinkle the demerara sugar on top. Bake in the preheated oven for 30 minutes, and then lower the oven temperature to 160°C/325°F/Gas Mark 3 and bake for a further 45 minutes.

4 When the cake is cooked, leave it in the tin for about 5 minutes and then turn out on to a cake rack to cool.

Pamela Stevens
Pangbourne, Berkshire

Preparation Time	20 minutes
Cooking Time	1¼ hours
Oven Temperature	180°C/350°F/Gas Mark 4, then
	160°C/325°F/Gas Mark 3

Reader's Tip

This cake can equally well be cooked in an 18 cm/7 inch round cake tin.

Christmas Cake

500 g/1 lb butter
250 g/8 oz plain flour, sifted
250 g/8 oz self-raising flour, sifted
375 g/12 oz soft brown sugar
1 teaspoon mixed spice
500 g/1 lb mixed dried fruit
1 teaspoon almond essence
1 teaspoon vanilla essence
6 eggs, beaten
demerara sugar, to sprinkle

1 Grease and line a 20 cm/8 inch deep-sided square cake tin with 3–4 sheets of greaseproof paper and baking parchment. Preheat the oven to 150°C/300°F/Gas Mark 2.

2 Rub the butter into the flour, and add the sugar, mixed spice, dried fruit, and the almond and vanilla essences. Then add the eggs and mix well. Spoon the mixture into the prepared tin. Sprinkle with demerara sugar.

3 Bake in the preheated oven for 2½–3 hours. Check after 2 hours, pushing a skewer into the middle of the cake. If it isn't cooked, put it back in the oven and check every 30 minutes until the skewer comes out clean.

Patricia Stockham
Honiton, Devon

Preparation Time	30 minutes
Cooking Time	2½–3 hours
Oven Temperature	150°C/300°F/Gas Mark 2

Reader's Tip

Don't overfill the tin – better to use two than to overfill one. Make this a few weeks before Christmas and brush it with brandy every few nights.

Guggy Fruit Cake

200 g/7 oz soft light brown sugar
175 g/6 oz sultanas
175 g/6 oz currants
250 ml/8 fl oz water
125 g/4 oz margarine
2 teaspoons mixed spice
300 g/10 oz self-raising flour, sifted

1 Grease and line a 20 cm/8 inch round, deep-sided cake tin and preheat the oven to 180°C/350°F/Gas Mark 4.

2 Put the sugar, dried fruit, water, margarine and mixed spice in a saucepan and heat gently to melt the margarine into the mixture. Leave to cool, then stir in the flour.

3 Transfer the cake mixture to the prepared cake tin and bake in the preheated oven for about 1 hour.

4 When the cake is cooked, turn it out on to a cake rack and allow to cool.

Anon

Preparation Time	20 minutes
Cooking Time	1 hour
Oven Temperature	180°C/350°F/Gas Mark 4

Reader's Tip

It is not necessary to slave for hours to produce wholesome and good-looking cakes. This recipe is simple and easy, and very quick to make.

Jenny Cake

125 g/4 oz granulated sugar
250 g/8 oz self-raising flour
375 g/12 oz mixed fruit
125 g/4 oz margarine, melted
4 medium eggs, beaten
150 ml/¼ pint milk
a pinch of nutmeg
1 teaspoon mixed spice

1 Grease and line a deep 18 cm/7 inch cake tin. Preheat the oven to 150°C/300°F/Gas Mark 2.

2 Put the sugar, flour and mixed fruit in a food processor and mix. Then add the margarine and eggs, and mix well. Add the cold milk and then the nutmeg and mixed spice.

3 Pour the cake mixture into the prepared cake tin and bake in the centre of the preheated oven for 2 hours 10 minutes.

4 Remove the cake from the oven and leave in the tin for about 30 minutes to cool slightly before turning out on to a cooling rack.

Eileen and Jenny
Wednesfield, Wolverhampton

Preparation Time	20 minutes
Cooking Time	2 hours 10 minutes
Oven Temperature	150°C/300°F/Gas Mark 2

Reader's Tip

Use as much nutmeg as you like. I tend to use a big pinch.

Mrs. Atherton's Loaf

65 ml/2½ fl oz water
250 g/8 oz mixed dried fruit
25 g/1 oz chopped nuts
65 g/2½ oz margarine
1 dessertspoon marmalade
50 g/2 oz soft brown sugar
½ teaspoon ground ginger
½ teaspoon mixed spice
1 egg
65 ml/2½ fl oz milk
½ teaspoon bicarbonate of soda
175 g/6 oz self-raising flour, sifted

1 Grease and line a 500 g/1 lb loaf tin. Preheat the oven to 180°C/350°F/Gas Mark 4.

2 Put the water, mixed dried fruit, chopped nuts, margarine, marmalade, soft brown sugar, ground ginger and mixed spice in a saucepan. Heat gently over a low heat and bring to the boil.

3 Remove the pan from the heat and then allow to stand for 2 minutes only. Now beat together until all the ingredients are mixed together well.

4 Stir in the egg, milk and bicarbonate of soda, and then stir in the flour.

5 Put the cake mixture in the prepared loaf tin and bake just above the centre of the preheated oven for about 45 minutes.

6 Insert the blade of a knife and if it comes out clean, the cake is cooked.

Elizabeth

'*This absolutely delicious cake came from a very modest reader who just gave me her first name and no address.*'

Preparation Time	20 minutes
Cooking Time	45 minutes
Oven Temperature	180°C/350°F/Gas Mark 4

Reader's Tip

If you want to make a larger, 1 kg/ 2 lb cake, double the quantities and use the appropriate loaf tin, and bake for 1–1¼ hours.

Small
Cakes &
Biscuits

Rock Cakes

125 g/4 oz margarine
250 g/8 oz self-raising flour, sifted
a pinch of salt
50 g/2 oz caster sugar
1 egg
a little milk

1 Grease a baking sheet and preheat the oven to 200°C/400°F/Gas Mark 6.

2 Rub the margarine into the flour and salt. Stir in the sugar. Mix in the egg and milk to make a soft dough.

3 Fork dollops of the mixture, about the size of a small egg, on to the prepared baking sheet. Sprinkle with a little caster sugar.

4 Bake in the preheated oven for 15–20 minutes until pale brown.

E. Ridout,
New Malden, Essex

	Makes 12–14 cakes, depending on size
Preparation Time	10 minutes
Cooking Time	15–20 minutes
Oven Temperature	200°C/400°F/Gas Mark 6

Reader's Tip

An optional extra is to include about 125 g/4 oz dried mixed fruit in the cake mixture.

Idiot Biscuits

75 g/3 oz butter, softened
50 g/2 oz caster sugar
½ teaspoon vanilla essence
125 g/4 oz plain flour, sifted
1 tablespoon cocoa powder, sifted

1 Lightly grease a baking sheet and preheat the oven to 160°C/325°F/Gas Mark 3.

2 Cream together the butter and sugar until pale and fluffy. Add the vanilla essence, and stir in the flour and cocoa powder.

3 Use your hands to bring the dough together. When the mixture is in one solid lump, roll into small balls. Arrange these on a baking sheet and press down lightly with a fork dipped in water (hot or cold).

4 Bake in the preheated oven for 20–30 minutes.

Jo Haines,
Great Dunmow, Essex

	Makes 16 biscuits
Preparation Time	15 minutes
Cooking Time	20–30 minutes
Oven Temperature	160°C/325°F/Gas Mark 3

Reader's Tip

Simply soften the butter by leaving it for a while at room temperature in a warm room. The obvious choice is the kitchen.

Fruit Scones

250 g/8 oz self-raising flour
½ teaspoon salt
40 g/1½ oz butter or margarine
50 g/2 oz sugar
50 g/2 oz sultanas or currants
about 150 ml/¼ pint milk

1 Grease a baking sheet and preheat the oven to 200°C/400°F/Gas Mark 6.

2 Sift together the flour and salt into a bowl, then add the butter or margarine, and crumble together until the mixture resembles fine breadcrumbs. Add the sugar and fruit and just enough milk to make a fairly stiff dough. Roll the dough into a ball.

3 Roll out on a floured surface until about 1 cm/½ inch thick, then cut into rounds with a 5 cm/2 inch cutter.

4 Arrange these on the prepared baking sheet and bake in the preheated oven for about 10–12 minutes.

5 When the scones are cool, cut them in half horizontally and butter.

Muriel Allan
Sunderland

'There is something very comforting
in cold weather about scones straight out
of the oven for tea. The recipe for these
scones has been in the family for
generations, and my Grandpa grew up
on them. We all love them too.'

	Makes 16 x 5 cm/2 in scones
Preparation Time	10 minutes
Cooking Time	10–12 minutes
Oven Temperature	200°C/400°F/Gas Mark 6

Reader's Tip

To make cheese scones, omit the sugar and fruit, and add 50–75 g/ 2–3 oz grated cooking cheese. For a glazed top, brush the scones with beaten egg before baking them. It is worth noting that scones freeze particularly well.

Crunchy Lemon Squares

150 g/5 oz caster sugar
150 g/5 oz self-raising flour, sifted
150 g/5 oz soft margarine
1 heaped teaspoon baking powder
grated rind and juice of 1 lemon
2–3 eggs, beaten, measured to 125 ml/4 fl oz
3 tablespoons granulated sugar

1 Grease and line an 18 x 23 x 2.5 cm/7 x 9 x 1 inch baking tray and preheat the oven to 180°C/350°F/ Gas Mark 4.

2 Put the caster sugar, flour, margarine, baking powder, lemon rind and eggs in a large mixing bowl and stir well to combine thoroughly.

3 Turn the mixture into the baking tray and smooth the surface. Bake in the centre of the preheated oven for about 30 minutes, until the cake is well risen and pale gold in colour and springs back when pressed in the centre.

4 Meanwhile, mix the lemon juice with the granulated sugar and spoon this over the cake while it is still hot. Leave in the baking tray until completely cold, then turn out and cut into 12 squares.

Angela Master
Royston, Hertfordshire

Preparation Time	25 minutes
Cooking Time	30 minutes
Oven Temperature	180°C/350°F/Gas Mark 4

Reader's Tip

This cake freezes well, if you'd like to save it for later.

Granny's Easter Biscuits

125 g/4 oz butter or margarine
75 g/3 oz caster sugar
2 egg yolks
250 g/8 oz self-raising flour
a pinch of mixed spice
a pinch of cinnamon
50 g/2 oz sultanas
1 egg white, beaten, for brushing
caster sugar, for sprinkling

1 Butter one or two baking sheets and preheat the oven to 180°C/350°F/Gas Mark 4.

2 Cream together the butter or margarine and sugar. Add the egg yolks, 1 at a time, and beat thoroughly. Add the flour, mixed spice, cinnamon and sultanas. Knead well.

3 Roll out on a floured board to about 5 mm/¼ inch thick. Cut into rounds with a 5 cm/2 inch cutter. Re-roll any leftover dough and cut again.

4 Place on the greased baking sheets, brush with egg white, and sprinkle with caster sugar.

5 Bake in the centre of the preheated oven for 10–15 minutes, until golden brown.

Mary Dyson
Truro, Cornwall

	Makes 20–25 biscuits
Preparation Time	15 minutes
Cooking Time	10–15 minutes
Oven Temperature	180°C/350°F/Gas Mark 4

Reader's Tip

This biscuit recipe is perfect for children – both to make and to eat.

Rich Fudge Brownies

125 g/4 oz plain chocolate
50 g/2 oz butter, chopped
2 medium eggs, beaten
175 g/6 oz caster sugar
1 teaspoon vanilla essence
75 g/3 oz self-raising flour, sifted
50 g/2 oz walnuts or pecan nuts, roughly chopped

1   Butter and line a 20 cm/8 inch square cake tin. Preheat the oven to 180°C/350°F/Gas Mark 4.

2   Melt the chocolate in a heatproof bowl over boiling water. Add the butter and stir until the butter is melted. Remove from the heat and allow to cool.

3   Add the eggs, caster sugar and vanilla essence and beat well.

4   Fold in the flour, using a large metal spoon. Then stir in the chopped nuts.

5   Pour the mixture into the prepared cake tin and bake for 25–40 minutes.

6   Allow to cool in the tin for 10 minutes. Then cut into squares and turn out on to a cooling rack.

Karin Smith
Reading, Berkshire

*'These chocolate brownies are
deliciously wicked and should be
administered on grey days when
only chocolate can help.'*

Preparation Time	15 minutes
Cooking Time	25–40 minutes
Oven Temperature	180°C/350°F/Gas Mark 4

Reader's Tip

Exactly how long you cook these brownies for depends on how you like them. If you like them very fudgy and gooey in the centre, cook them for just 25 minutes. If you like them firm and dry, cook them for longer. You can also add plain, milk or white chocolate chunks,

Chocolate Goodies

125 g/4 oz digestive biscuits
125 g/4 oz margarine
1 tablespoon caster sugar
1 tablespoon golden syrup
3 tablespoons chocolate powder
a handful of sultanas
plain cooking chocolate

1 Grease a large baking sheet

2 Put the digestive biscuits in a polythene bag and crush them roughly with a rolling pin until they form large crumbs.

3 Melt the margarine, add all the remaining ingredients except for the chocolate, and mix well.

4 Press the biscuit mixture firmly on to the greased baking sheet. Allow to set in the refrigerator for at least 1 hour.

5 Meanwhile, melt the chocolate and pour over the set biscuit mixture. Return to the refrigerator to set and cut into pieces when cooled.

Mary Dyson
Truro, Cornwall

Preparation Time	15 minutes
🧁 **Reader's Tip**	If you like dates, use chopped dates instead of sultanas. Another possibility is to use a mixture of sultanas and dates.

Granny's Biscuits

125 g/4 oz hard margarine
1 dessertspoon golden syrup
125 g/4 oz self-raising flour
50 g/2 oz porridge oats
$\frac{1}{2}$ teaspoon bicarbonate of soda
75 g/3 oz demerara sugar
$\frac{1}{2}$ teaspoon mixed spice

1 Grease a baking sheet and preheat the oven to 180°C/350°F/Gas Mark 4.

2 Melt the margarine and syrup in a saucepan. Pour this on to all the other ingredients in a mixing bowl, and mix well.

3 Roll the biscuit dough into small balls and flatten these on a baking sheet, allowing enough room for them to expand.

4 Bake in the preheated oven for 10–15 minutes and leave to cool slightly before removing them from the tray.

Pam Whitwam
Reading, Berkshire

	Makes 16–18 biscuits
Preparation Time	5 minutes
Cooking Time	10–15 minutes
Oven Temperature	180°C/350°F/Gas Mark 4

Reader's Tip

This is a very easy recipe and therefore a good one for children to make, as long as help is given with pouring the hot margarine and syrup into the mixing bowl.

Easy Eccles Cakes

375 g/12 oz puff pastry, thawed if frozen
25 g/1 oz granulated sugar

FILLING
1 tablespoon melted butter
125 g/4 oz soft brown sugar
125 g/4 oz currants or seedless raisins
1/2 teaspoon cinnamon
1/4 teaspoon ground nutmeg
50 g/2 oz candied peel
grated rind of 1 lemon

1 Grease a baking tray and preheat the oven to 230°C/
450°F/Gas Mark 8.

2 Roll out the pastry thinly and cut into 12 cm/5 inch
squares.

3 Mix together all the filling ingredients
and place a heaped teaspoon of
this mixture in the centre of each
pastry square. Lightly damp the
pastry edges, bring the edges up
to the centre and pinch together.

4 Turn the parcels over and
mould them into round
shapes. Roll with a rolling pin until
the cakes are about 6 cm/2½ inches in
diameter and the fruit shows through the pastry.

5 Repeat until all the ingredients have been used up. Dampen the tops and sprinkle with the sugar.

6 Place all the cakes on the prepared baking tray and cut three slits in the top of each one. Bake in the preheated oven for 10–15 minutes until lightly browned.

Pam Whitwam
Reading, Berkshire

'I think these are nostalgia cakes. They are what we had at Granny's when we were little.'

Preparation Time	20 minutes
Cooking Time	10–15 minutes
Oven Temperature	230°C/450°F/Gas Mark 8

Reader's Tip

Eccles cakes may also be made using flaky or rough puff pastry, as you prefer. Either way, they're delicious.

Mock Florentine Bars

175 g/6 oz plain chocolate
125 g/4 oz soft margarine
175 g/6 oz caster sugar
2 eggs
125 g/4 oz glacé cherries, chopped
125 g/4 oz sultanas
150 g/5 oz porridge oats
75 g/3 oz desiccated coconut

1 Grease and line a 23 × 33 cm/9 × 13 inch Swiss roll tin with greaseproof paper, or use a 20 cm/ 8 inch square tin. Preheat the oven to 180°C/350°F/Gas Mark 4.

2 Melt the chocolate in a basin over a pan of hot water, then spread this evenly over the paper in the tin. Chill until the chocolate has set.

3 Cream together the margarine and sugar until light and fluffy. Gradually add the eggs, beating well after each addition.

4 Mix in the cherries, sultanas, oats and desiccated coconut. Spread this mixture over the chocolate.

5 Bake in the centre of the preheated oven for 25–35 minutes until golden brown. Leave in the tin until completely cold, then invert on to a board, peel off the paper and cut into 24 bars.

Judy Cairns
Hemdon, Northamptonshire

'These are good served with coffee after dinner and more original than a box of After Eights.'

Makes 24 bars

Preparation Time 15 minutes
Cooking Time 25–35 minutes
Oven Temperature 180°C/350°F/Gas Mark 4

Reader's Tip

Use a plain chocolate that has at least 70% cocoa solids. You will find the percentage of cocoa solids stated on the wrapper. If these biscuits fall apart when you cut them, put the whole block in the freezer until they are hard enough to cut more easily.

Chocolate Cakes

Chocolate Cake with Orange Syrup

200 g/7 oz self-raising flour
2 tablespoons drinking chocolate powder
250 g/8 oz caster sugar
¾ teaspoon salt
125 g/4 oz soft margarine or butter
1 teaspoon vanilla essence
2 eggs, beaten with 175 ml/6 fl oz milk

SYRUP
rind and juice of 1 orange
125 g/4 oz sugar

1 Grease and line an oblong 1 kg/2 lb loaf tin. Preheat the oven to 180°C/350°F/Gas Mark 4.

2 Sift together the flour, drinking chocolate, sugar and salt.

3 Rub in the margarine or butter.

4 Add the vanilla essence and milk, and beat well.

5 Pour the cake mixture into the prepared loaf tin and bake in the preheated oven for about 1 hour.

6 To make the orange syrup, put the orange rind and juice and the sugar in a pan, bring to the boil and continue to boil until the mixture is thick.

7 While the cake is still hot, make slits across the top of the cake and pour over the orange syrup. Allow to cool completely before turning out on to a plate.

Lindsey Appleby
Reading, Berkshire

'The flavours of chocolate and orange are perfect partners.'

Preparation Time	20 minutes
Cooking Time	1 hour
Oven Temperature	180°C/350°F/Gas Mark 4

Reader's Tip

This is quite a wet cake mixture, so be sure not to use a loose-bottomed cake tin.

One-Bowl Chocolate Cake

125 g/4 oz butter, softened
125 g/4 oz caster sugar
125 g/4 oz self-raising flour, sifted
2 tablespoons drinking chocolate
1 teaspoon cocoa
1 teaspoon baking powder
2 eggs
2 tablespoons cold milk
$^1/_2$ teaspoon vanilla essence

1 Grease and line two 15 cm/6 in cake tins and preheat the oven to 190°C/375°F/Gas Mark 5.

2 Put all the ingredients in a food processor and whizz until smooth.

3 Turn the cake mixture into the prepared cake tins and bake in the preheated oven for 20–30 minutes or until well risen, firm to the touch and beginning to shrink away from the sides.

4 Turn the cake out on to a cooling rack and allow it to cool.

Heather Baker
Bognor Regis, West Sussex

Preparation Time	20 minutes
Cooking Time	20–30 minutes
Oven Temperature	190°C/375°F/Gas Mark 5

Reader's Tip

To use this mixture for fairy cakes, increase the oven temperature to 200°C/400°F/Gas Mark 6 and reduce the cooking time to 15–20 minutes.

Chocolate Biscuit Cake

1 tablespoon golden syrup
150 g/5 oz butter
1 tablespoon sugar
2 tablespoons cocoa powder
275 g/9 oz digestive biscuits, crushed
25 g/1 oz ground almonds
2 teaspoons coffee essence
25 g/1 oz sultanas (optional)

1 Grease a shallow oven tray.

2 Place the golden syrup in a saucepan with the butter and sugar, and warm gently over low heat. Remove from the heat and then add the cocoa, biscuit crumbs, ground almonds, coffee essence and sultanas, if using.

3 Press the mixture into the prepared oven tray, using the back of a spoon. Refrigerate for a few hours and then slice.

Anne Larpent
Ross-on-Wye, Herefordshire

Preparation Time   10 minutes

Reader's Tip

If you have a food processor, crush the biscuits and then add all the other ingredients and whizz until the mixture comes together. This cake freezes well, in which case it should be thawed at room temperature for 2–3 hours before eating. A finishing touch is to melt 75 g/3 oz plain chocolate and pour it evenly over the cake to set – millions of calories but absolutely wonderful.

One-Stage Chocolate Cake

125 g/4 oz soft margarine
150 g/5 oz caster sugar
150 g/5 oz self-raising flour
1 tablespoon cocoa powder
2 large eggs
2 tablespoons milk
1/2 teaspoon vanilla essence

FILLING
50 g/2 oz soft margarine
50 g/2 oz icing sugar
50 g/2 oz drinking chocolate

1 Grease and line two round sandwich cake tins and preheat the oven to 200°C/400°F/Gas Mark 6.

2 Put all the ingredients in a bowl and blend together with an electric mixer. Pour into the cake tins, smooth over the tops and bake in the preheated oven for 15 minutes, until risen and firm to the touch. Run a knife around the tins and tip upside down on to a cooling rack.

3 Meanwhile, mix together all the filling ingredients with a wooden spoon until soft and creamy. When the cake is cool, sandwich the cakes with half the filling and spread the rest on top of the cake.

Anne Dean
Altrincham, Cheshire

Preparation Time	20 minutes
Cooking Time	15 minutes
Oven Temperature	200°C/400°F/Gas Mark 6

Reader's Tip

An alternative filling, if you prefer, is to use jam – in any flavour that you really like.

Chocolate Truffle Cake

475 g/15 oz plain chocolate
100 g/3½ oz butter
150 g/5 oz caster sugar
2 teaspoons coffee granules
4 eggs, separated
40 g/1½ oz plain flour
25 g/1 oz toasted ground hazelnuts

1 Grease and line a 22 cm/8½ inch cake tin. Preheat the oven to 160°C/325°F/Gas Mark 3.

2 Melt the chocolate in a bain-marie. Cream together the butter and sugar.

3 Dissolve the coffee in warm water. Beat together the coffee, the butter mixture, the chocolate and the 4 egg yolks.

4 Whisk the egg whites and fold into the mixture. Fold in the flour and nuts.

5 Bake in the preheated oven for 1¼ hours.

Ann Meddings
Kingston, Surrey

Preparation Time	20 minutes
Cooking Time	1¼ hours
Oven Temperature	160°C/325°F/Gas Mark 3

Reader's Tip

As always, use the best-quality plain chocolate, with at least 70% cocoa solids. Less then that will not achieve such good results.

Foolproof Chocolate Cake

250 g/8 oz self-raising flour
25 g/1 oz cocoa powder
½ teaspoon salt
125 g/4 oz butter or hard margarine, softened
200 g/7 oz caster sugar
3 eggs
5 tablespoons water
5 tablespoons condensed milk
½ teaspoon vanilla essence

1 Grease and line two shallow 18 cm/7 inch cake tins. Preheat the oven to 180°C/350°F/Gas Mark 4.

2 Sift together the flour, cocoa powder and salt. Rub in the butter or margarine until the mixture looks like fine breadcrumbs, with no big lumps. Stir in the sugar.

3 In another bowl, beat together the eggs, water, condensed milk and vanilla essence. Pour this mixture into the flour mixture and mix until there are no dry bits visible.

4 Pour the cake mixture into the prepared cake tins and bake in the preheated oven for about 25–30 minutes. Remove from the oven and leave for 10 minutes before turning out on to a cake rack to cool completely.

5 Sandwich the cakes together with jam, butter cream or whipped fresh cream, as you prefer. A nice finishing touch is to pour melted chocolate over the cake, if liked.

Helen Kaczmarczuk
Dunstable, Bedfordshire

'This recipe cannot fail. A perfect quick birthday cake.'

Preparation Time	15 minutes
Cooking Time	25–30 minutes
Oven Temperature	180°C/350°F/Gas Mark 4

Reader's Tip

Be sure that you use cocoa powder – not drinking chocolate – to make this recipe. It's so much better.

American Chocolate Cake

300 g/10 oz self-raising flour
$^1/_2$ teaspoon salt
3 tablespoons cocoa
175 g/6 oz caster sugar
1 teaspoon bicarbonate of soda
300 ml/$^1/_2$ pint milk
150 ml/$^1/_4$ pint corn oil
1 tablespoon golden syrup
3 teaspoons vanilla essence

CHOCOLATE ICING
40 g/1$^1/_2$ oz butter
25 g/1 oz cocoa, sifted
3 tablespoons milk
125 g/4 oz icing sugar

1 Grease and line two 20 cm/8 inch sandwich tins with greased greaseproof paper. Preheat the oven to 180°C/350°F/Gas Mark 4.

2 Sift the flour, salt, cocoa and sugar into a mixing bowl and make a well in the centre.

3 Dissolve the bicarbonate of soda in 1 tablespoon of the milk and pour this into the well, with the remaining milk, oil, golden syrup and vanilla essence, and beat well to make a smooth batter.

4 Pour the cake mixture into the prepared cake tins and bake in the preheated oven for about 35–40 minutes, or until the cakes spring back when lightly pressed with a fingertip.

5 Meanwhile, make the chocolate icing. Melt the butter in a small saucepan and stir in the cocoa, and cook over a low heat for 1 minute. Remove from the heat and add the milk and icing sugar. Beat well to mix and then leave to cool, stirring occasionally until the icing has thickened to a spreading consistency.

6 When the cakes are cooked, turn them out on to a wire cooling rack and leave to cool.

7 Sandwich the two cakes together with chocolate icing, and put more icing on top of the cake.

Anon

'Administer this cake to chocoholics — liberally and frequently.'

Preparation Time	10 minutes
Cooking Time	35–40 minutes
Oven Temperature	180°C/350°F/Gas Mark 4

Reader's Tip

Sunflower oil will work just as well as corn oil if that is what you have in your kitchen cupboard.

Pfister Cake

150 g/5 oz butter
265 g/8¹/₂ oz caster sugar
5 eggs, separated
150 g/5 oz ground almonds
150 g/5 oz dark chocolate, broken into very small pieces
100 g/3¹/₂ oz self-raising flour, sifted

1 Grease and line a 20 cm/8 inch cake tin and preheat the oven to 180°C/350°F/Gas Mark 4.

2 Beat together the butter and sugar until white.

3 Add the egg yolks and almonds, then add the chocolate pieces and mix well. Fold in the flour.

4 Beat the egg whites until stiff, then fold into the mixture, using a metal spoon. Mix well but do not beat.

5 Put the mixture in the prepared cake tin and bake in the preheated oven for 50 minutes–1 hour.

6 Turn out on to a cooling rack and allow to cool completely.

Betty Jones
Cyncoed, Cardiff

Preparation Time	20 minutes
Cooking Time	50 minutes–1 hour
Oven Temperature	180°C/350°F/Gas Mark 4

Reader's Tip

Store this cake in aluminium foil for at least a week before serving. It gets better and better!

Chocolate Orange Chip Cake

125 g/4 oz butter or margarine
125 g/4 oz caster sugar
1 tablespoon grated orange rind
2 eggs
150 g/5 oz self-raising flour, sifted
1 tablespoon chopped chocolate or chocolate chips
50 g/2 oz walnuts
1 tablespoon orange juice

1 Grease and line an 18 cm/7 inch cake tin and preheat the oven to 180°C/350°F/Gas Mark 4.

2 Place the butter or margarine, sugar and orange rind in a mixing bowl. Beat for 3 minutes until light and fluffy.

3 Add the eggs, 1 at a time, and beat for 1 minute more.

4 Add the flour, chocolate, nuts and orange juice, and mix well.

5 Turn the mixture into the prepared cake tin and bake in the preheated oven for 25–30 minutes until the cake springs back when touched lightly.

Miss J.C. Turner
Hook, Hampshire

Preparation Time	15 minutes
Cooking Time	25–30 minutes
Oven Temperature	180°C/350°F/Gas Mark 4

Reader's Tip

Chocolate and orange are a great combination of flavours made in heaven.

Chocolate Mosaic

250 g/8 oz rich tea biscuits
3 tablespoons chocolate spread
2 tablespoons golden syrup
50 g/2 oz butter
$\frac{1}{2}$ teaspoon ground ginger
2 eggs
150 ml/$\frac{1}{4}$ pint double cream
grated chocolate, to decorate

1 Grease and line a 500 g/1 lb loaf tin with clingfilm, making sure it comes up and over the sides.

2 Place the biscuits in a plastic bag and crush into small pieces with a rolling pin.

3 Put the chocolate spread, golden syrup, butter and ground ginger in a saucepan, and blend them together over a gentle heat.

4 Whisk the eggs and add to the chocolate mixture, stirring well as the eggs cook to keep the mixture really smooth.

5 Remove from the heat and stir in the biscuit pieces, making sure that they are evenly coated.

6 Press the mixture into the prepared loaf tin and place in the refrigerator for several hours, preferably overnight.

7 Meanwhile, whip the double cream until stiff.

8 Turn out the chocolate cake, cover with whipped cream and decorate with grated chocolate.

Pat Brown
Reading, Berkshire

'This is simple and quick to make, yet rich and impressive.'

Preparation Time	20 minutes

 **Reader's Tip**

For a finer finish, crush the biscuits in a food processor and then add all the melted ingredients.

Chocolate Cake

125 g/4 oz hard margarine
125 g/4 oz soft brown sugar
2 tablespoons golden syrup
175 g/6 oz self-raising flour
125 g/4 oz cocoa
1 egg
150 ml/¼ pint milk
½ teaspoon bicarbonate of soda

1 Grease and line two 20 cm/8 inch sandwich tins. Preheat the oven to 190°C/375°F/Gas Mark 5.

2 Melt the margarine, sugar and syrup in a saucepan over a gentle heat. Transfer to a large mixing bowl and pour over the flour and cocoa. Mix together well. Add the egg and stir again.

3 Warm the milk slightly, stir in the bicarbonate of soda and pour this on to the other ingredients, which will now be very runny.

4 Pour the cake mixture into the prepared cake tins and bake in the preheated oven for about 30 minutes. Turn out on to a cooling rack and allow to cool.

Pam Whitwam
Reading, Berkshire

Preparation Time	15 minutes
Cooking Time	30 minutes
Oven Temperature	190°C/375°F/Gas Mark 5

Reader's Tip

Sandwich the cakes together with chocolate or coffee butter icing. On special occasions, top with chocolate icing and walnuts.

Chocolate Walnut Cake

250 g/8 oz plain chocolate
250 g/8 oz butter or margarine
2 eggs
2 tablespoons caster sugar
250 g/8 oz digestive biscuits
40 g/1¹/₂ oz chopped walnuts, plus a little extra to decorate
40 g/1¹/₂ oz glacé cherries, plus a few extra, halved, to decorate
1 tablespoon brandy or rum

1 Butter an 18 cm/7 inch cake tin with a removable base.

2 Melt the chocolate in a bowl over a pan of boiling water. While the chocolate is softening, melt the butter or margarine in another pan.

3 Beat the eggs and add the caster sugar. Pour the melted butter into the egg mixture in a steady stream, stirring continuously. Add the melted chocolate and beat this in.

4 Break the digestive biscuits into small pieces, and stir these into the mixture. Then add the walnuts, the glacé cherries, and the brandy or rum.

5 Transfer the mixture to the prepared cake tin, and decorate with the reserved walnuts and glacé cherries. Refrigerate until needed.

Gloria Cann
White Waltham, Berkshire

Preparation Time   15 minutes

Reader's Tip

One of the joys of this cake is that it does not require any cooking. Simply refrigerate it until ready to serve.

Quick Chocolate Cake

125 g/4 oz self-raising flour
25 g/1 oz cocoa or carob powder
150 g/5 oz caster sugar
150 g/5 oz soft margarine
3 eggs
1 teaspoon baking powder
1 tablespoon hot water

CHOCOLATE FILLING AND TOPPING
200 g/7 oz cooking chocolate or carob bar
2 tablespoons milk

1 Grease and line two 18 cm/7 inch sandwich tins. Preheat the oven to 180°C/350°F/Gas Mark 4.

2 Sieve the flour and cocoa or carob powder into a mixing bowl. Add all the other ingredients and beat well until smooth and shiny.

3 Divide the cake mixture between the two prepared sandwich tins and bake in the preheated oven for 25–30 minutes until the cakes spring back when they are touched lightly.

4 Meanwhile, make the chocolate filling and topping. Cut the chocolate into small pieces and place it, or the carob powder, in a bowl over a pan of hot water to melt. Remove from the heat and add the milk, 1 tablespoon at a time, until the mixture thickens.

5 When the cake is cooked, turn out on to a cooling rack and allow to cool. Sandwich and top the cake with the prepared chocolate filling and topping.

Miss J.C. Turner
Hook, Hampshire

'This recipe is easy to make, quick to cook, and tends to disappear rapidly from the plate.'

Preparation Time	20 minutes
Cooking Time	25–30 minutes
Oven Temperature	180°C/350°F/Gas Mark 4

Reader's Tip

Chocolate does not agree with everybody and some people are actually allergic to it. Carob, which comes from the carob tree that grows all over the Mediterranean and in the US, is considered by some people to be a healthier alternative – high in vitamins and minerals, and free from caffeine.

Summer Cake

125 g/4 oz margarine
1 tablespoon golden syrup
1 tablespoon sugar
1¹/₂ tablespoons cocoa
75 g/3 oz cornflakes

1 Grease a shallow 18 cm/7 inch cake tin, and line the greased tin with clingfilm so that it will be easy to remove the cake.

2 Slowly melt the margarine with the syrup and sugar in a large saucepan.

3 Stir in the cocoa, then add the cornflakes and stir well.

4 Transfer the cake mixture to the prepared cake tin and leave to set in the refrigerator.

Lindy Moffatt
Hadlow Down, Sussex

Preparation Time   15 minutes

Reader's Tip

This is an excellent recipe to start children off in the kitchen. You can experiment with their different favourite breakfast cereals and discover which works best. You can also, if you prefer, use individual cup cases instead of a large cake tin.

Biscuit Cake

250 g/8 oz rich tea biscuits
125 g/4 oz margarine
2 teaspoons cocoa
1–2 tablespoons golden syrup
1 tablespoon caster sugar
50 g/2 oz sultanas
125 g/4 oz plain chocolate

1 Grease and line an 18 cm/7 inch or 20 cm/8 inch cake tin with clingfilm, so that it comes up over the sides of the tin.

2 Crush the biscuits by putting them in a polythene bag and pressing with a rolling pin. They can be crushed as coarsely or as finely as you like.

3 Put the margarine, cocoa, golden syrup, sugar and sultanas in a large saucepan. Heat over a gentle heat and bring to the boil, then mix in the biscuits.

4 Press the mixture into the prepared cake tin. Melt the chocolate in a bowl over hot water and then pour over the cake. Leave to set in the refrigerator. Just before serving, simply peel away the clingfilm to reveal your perfect cake.

Lindy Moffatt
Hadlow Down, Sussex

Preparation Time   15 minutes

🧁 *Reader's Tip*

This biscuit cake is very easy to prepare, and makes an excellent pudding. Serve with cream.

Chocolate Loaf

vegetable oil, for greasing
175 g/6 oz plain cooking chocolate, broken into small pieces
50 ml/2 fl oz dark rum
175 g/6 oz unsalted butter, softened
1 teaspoon sugar
2 eggs, separated
125 g/4 oz ground almonds
75 g/3 oz hazelnuts or almonds, crushed
$^1/_3$ teaspoon salt
300 ml/$^1/_2$ pint double cream, whipped, to cover

1 Line a 1.5 kg/3 lb loaf tin or a 20 cm/8 inch round cake tin with greaseproof paper, leaving some of the paper overlapping the tin. Then grease the paper with the vegetable oil and stand the tin upside down on kitchen paper to drain.

2 Melt the chocolate in a basin over hot water, stirring continuously. Then stir in the rum. Remove from the heat and set aside to cool.

3 In a large bowl, cream together the butter and sugar, using a wooden spoon, until smooth and pale. Beat in the egg yolks and ground almonds. Then add the chocolate mixture and beat again. Mix in the crushed nuts.

4 Whisk the egg whites with the salt until they form stiff peaks.

5 Using a metal spoon, carefully fold the egg whites into the chocolate mixture.

6 Spoon the cake mixture into the prepared loaf tin and spread out evenly with a palette knife.

7 Cover the tin with aluminium foil and put in the refrigerator to chill for at least 5 hours or until the loaf is firm, preferably overnight.

8 To unmould the loaf, loosen the sides with a knife and quickly dip the tin into hot water. Turn out the cake over a serving plate.

9 Cover with cream and slice the loaf thinly.

Delia Gaze
Deptford, London

'This is a good alternative to Christmas Cake for those who do not like fruit cake.'

Preparation Time	40 minutes, plus at least 5 hours chilling time
Reader's Tip	If you have a microwave, this is the perfect way to melt the chocolate.

Karolyi Torta

8 eggs, separated
200 g/7 oz icing sugar
150 g/5 oz best quality plain chocolate, broken into pieces
140 g/4½ oz slightly salted butter
2–4 tablespoons lukewarm water
1 tablespoon Tia Maria
15 g/½ oz vanilla sugar
150 g/5 oz ground hazelnuts or almonds

FILLING AND TOPPING
425 g/14 oz apricot preserve
1–2 tablespoons Cointreau
300 ml/½ pint whipping cream
15 g/½ oz vanilla sugar
1 tablespoon icing sugar
125 g/4 oz chocolate
25 g/1 oz butter
1–2 tablespoons Tia Maria
a pinch of instant coffee

1 Line two large round baking tins with greaseproof paper. Preheat the oven to 150°C/300°F/Gas Mark 2.

2 Beat the egg whites until they are just beginning to stiffen, then add about one-third of the icing sugar, bit by bit, until the egg whites just hold their shape.

3 Melt the broken chocolate pieces with the butter, 1–2 tablespoons lukewarm water and the Tia Maria in a bowl over hot water.

4 Beat the egg yolks with the remaining sugar, the vanilla sugar and 1–2 tablespoons lukewarm water until thick and frothy. Slowly add the cooled chocolate and butter mixture, and add the ground nuts. Then carefully fold in the egg whites.

5 Pour the cake mixture into the prepared cake tins and bake for about 40–50 minutes, or until a metal skewer inserted into the centre comes out clean. Allow the cake to cool in the tin, then turn out on to a cooling rack.

6 Mix the apricot preserve with the Cointreau, and spread the cakes with this mixture.

7 Beat the cream, gradually adding the two sugars as it stiffens.

8 Melt the chocolate and butter in a bowl over hot water. Add the Tia Maria and instant coffee.

9 Sandwich the cakes together with some of the cream, then pile the rest on top and sides of the cake. Swirl the melted chocolate through the cream with the prongs of a fork to make a pretty pattern.

Elisabeth Wengersky
South Hampstead, London

'Choose a really superior apricot jam, with at least 40% fruit.'

Preparation Time	30 minutes
Cooking Time	40–50 minutes
Oven Temperature	150°C/300°F/Gas Mark 2

 **Reader's Tip**

For the best flavour, keep this delicious Hungarian cake in the refrigerator for 1 day before eating. It can also be frozen for up to 2 weeks.

Party
Cakes

Auntie Glad's Bakewell Tart

125 g/4 oz shortcrust pastry (thawed if frozen)
raspberry jam, to taste, for spreading
275 g/9 oz ground rice
275 g/9 oz caster sugar
275 g/9 oz butter, softened, or soft margarine
3 eggs
$\frac{1}{2}$ teaspoon almond essence
a little cold water or milk (optional)

1 Grease three deep 18 cm/7 inch pie plates – one to eat and two to freeze, though they are unlikely to stay in the freezer for very long before prying fingers have raided it. Preheat the oven to 200°C/400°F/Gas Mark 6.

2 Roll the shortcrust pastry thinly and line the pie plates with it. Spread the pastry as thinly or as thickly as you like with raspberry jam.

3 Beat together the ground rice, caster sugar, butter or margarine, eggs and almond essence to a smooth paste. If the mixture is too stiff, add a little cold water or milk, as you prefer.

4 Divide the mixture between the three tins and smooth the surface with a palette knife.

5 Bake in the preheated oven for about 30 minutes or until the pastry is golden brown and the filling is firm to the touch.

6 Serve hot or cold with custard or cream.

Rev. Raymond Smith
Shrewsbury, Shropshire

'Here is a recipe that really DOES work and is absolutely gorgeous. There was a lovely old lady in one of my first churches who was as far round as she was high and had a highly polished black leaded grate on which she cooked the most divine cakes and pastries. I got this recipe from her and after our first son was born she became "Auntie Glad" — hence the name of the recipe.'

Preparation Time	20 minutes
Cooking Time	30 minutes
Oven Temperature	200°C/400°F/Gas Mark 6

Reader's Tip

This recipe uses ground rice rather than ground almonds — this is a lot cheaper and tastes just as good provided, of course, that you don't forget to add the almond essence.

Whisky Cake

175g/6 oz sultanas
125 g/4 oz butter
125 g/4 oz caster sugar
1 egg
1 teaspoon bicarbonate of soda
175 g/6 oz plain flour
$\frac{1}{2}$ teaspoon grated nutmeg
65 g/2$\frac{1}{2}$ oz chopped walnuts
1 tablespoon lemon juice
1 tablespoon whisky

1 Grease and line a 20 cm/8 inch deep-sided cake tin and preheat the oven to 180°C/350°F/Gas Mark 4.

2 Simmer the sultanas in just enough water to cover for 5–10 minutes. Drain and reserve the cooking liquid.

3 Beat together the butter and sugar until fluffy. Beat in the egg.

4 Add the bicarbonate of soda to the flour and sieve into the cake mixture with the nutmeg, cooled sultanas, walnuts, lemon juice and whisky.

5 Put the mixture into the prepared cake tin and bake in the preheated oven for 45–55 minutes.

Jean Hurley
Ashcombe, Devon

Preparation Time	20 minutes
Cooking Time	45–55 minutes
Oven Temperature	180°C/350°F/Gas Mark 4

Reader's Tip

If the mixture seems a little dry, add some of the sultana cooking liquid.

Treacle Cake

300 g/10 oz self-raising flour, sifted
200 g/7 oz caster sugar
165 g/5½ oz mixed dried fruit
1 egg, beaten
250 ml/8 fl oz milk
2 tablespoons black treacle

1 Grease and line a 1 kg/2 lb loaf tin with greaseproof paper. Preheat the oven to 180°C/350°F/Gas Mark 4.

2 Put the flour, sugar and dried fruit in a large mixing bowl. Make a well in the centre and mix in the egg and milk.

3 Add the black treacle and mix in thoroughly.

4 Pour the cake mixture into the prepared cake tin. Bake for 1¼ hours until a knife inserted into the centre comes out clean.

Lindy Moffatt
Hadlow Down, Sussex

Preparation Time	15 minutes
Cooking Time	1¼ hours
Oven Temperature	180°C/350°F/Gas Mark 4

Reader's Tip

You can use golden syrup instead of black treacle. This is rather sweeter but not so rich and will give a slightly lighter flavour.

Black Forest Gateau

1 heaped tablespoon cocoa powder
2 tablespoons hot water
175 g/6 oz caster sugar
175 g/6 oz soft margarine
3 medium eggs
175 g/6 oz self-raising flour, sifted

TO ASSEMBLE
a little Kirsch
morello cherry jam
whipped cream
125 g/4 oz dark chocolate

1 Grease and line two 18 cm/7 inch cake tins. Preheat the oven to 160°C/325°F/Gas Mark 3.

2 Blend the cocoa with the hot water and allow to cool.

3 Cream together the sugar and margarine, preferably using an electric hand mixer, until the mixture becomes white and fluffy. Then add the cocoa mixture.

4 Beat in the first egg and, as you work, stop beating a few times and scrape the mixture from the sides of the bowl. Add a little flour with the second and third eggs to prevent curdling. Then fold in the remaining flour, using a metal tablespoon.

5 Divide the mixture between the two prepared cake tins and smooth over gently using a knife. Bake on the middle shelf of the preheated oven for 20–30 minutes, until the cake is firm, golden brown, and shrinking away slightly from the sides of the tin. Turn out on to a cooling rack and allow to cool completely.

6 Cut the two cakes through the middle horizontally and sprinkle on a little Kirsch. Sandwich the two cake halves together with cherry jam. Put the two cakes together with whipped cream between them. Decorate the top with more whipped cream and grate chocolate over the top, using a cheese grater.

Mary Gillies
Ryde, Isle of Wight

'Black Forest Gateau has become the laughing stock of cakes, but most people secretly love it. Tell them it's a 70s retro feast and they'll tuck in.'

Preparation Time	20–30 minutes
Cooking Time	20–30 minutes
Oven Temperature	160°C/325°F/Gas Mark 3

Reader's Tip

When you are folding in the flour, hold the tablespoon loosely or you will find yourself stirring instead of folding. If the cake seems to be dry or overcooked, moisten it with the juice from a tin of fruit, or sprinkle with a few drops of Kirsch, Amaretto or Cointreau.

Sticky Macaroon Cake

50 g/2 oz soft margarine
125 g/4 oz caster sugar
125 g/4 oz desiccated coconut
1 large egg
3 drops vanilla essence
50 g/2 oz sultanas
50 g/2 oz glacé cherries, chopped
25 g/1 oz walnuts, chopped
25 g/1 oz dried pineapple, chopped
25 g/1 oz dried papaya, chopped
16 squares of plain cooking chocolate
chopped walnuts, to decorate

1 Grease and line a 20 cm/8 inch sandwich cake tin with baking parchment. Preheat the oven to 180°C/350°F/Gas Mark 4.

2 Mix together the margarine, sugar, coconut, egg and vanilla essence. Then add the sultanas, cherries, walnuts, pineapple and papaya.

3 When all the ingredients are well mixed, divide the mixture between the two prepared cake tins and press down with the back of a fork. Bake in the preheated oven for 20 minutes, or until the top looks golden brown.

4 Remove the cakes from the oven and gently run the blade of a knife around the edge of the tins. Carefully invert the cakes on to two suitable size plates. The cake will look pale and slightly sticky. Leave it to cool.

5 When the cake is cold, melt the chocolate and cover the pale side of the cake. Scatter with chopped walnuts while the chocolate is still warm.

Doreen Williamson
Hull, East Yorkshire

'This unusual cake is sinfully sticky — guaranteed there won't be anything left on the plate.'

Preparation Time	30 minutes
Cooking Time	20 minutes
Oven Temperature	180°C/350°F/Gas Mark 4

Reader's Tip

This cake can be made a day or two in advance before you decorate it with chocolate and walnuts.

Walnut Cake

75 g/3 oz *walnuts*
175 g/6 oz *margarine*
175 g/6 oz *caster sugar*
3 *eggs*
175 g/6 oz *self-raising flour, sifted*

BUTTER CREAM
75 g/3 oz *butter*
175 g/6 oz *icing sugar, sifted*
1–2 *tablespoons lemon juice*

1 Grease and line two shallow 18 cm/7 inch cake tins.
Preheat the oven to 180°C/350°F/Gas Mark 4.

2 In a food processor or blender, process the walnuts,
reserving 9 walnut halves for decorating the cake.

3 In the food processor or blender, mix the margarine
and sugar until creamy, then add the eggs, and then
the ground walnuts and flour.

4 Transfer the cake mixture to the two prepared tins and
bake in the preheated oven for 20 minutes. Then turn
out the cakes and place on a wire cooling rack.

5 Meanwhile, make the butter cream. Cream together
the butter and icing sugar, adding the lemon juice to
obtain a creamy consistency.

6 Sandwich the two cakes with the prepared butter icing and spread some more on the top. Decorate with the reserved walnut halves.

Griselda Hobson
London

'Walnut cake is an acquired taste and yes, I have acquired it.'

Preparation Time	20 minutes
Cooking Time	20 minutes
Oven Temperature	180°C/350°F/Gas Mark 4

Reader's Tip

Do not be tempted to use margarine to make the butter cream – it will not be nearly as good as if you use butter. Another idea is to omit the walnuts and to add a drop or two of vanilla essence instead. Then sandwich the two cakes with strawberries and whipped cream.

Rice Cake

250 g/8 oz butter, softened
250 g/8 oz sugar
3 eggs
75 g/3 oz self-raising flour, sifted
150 g/5 oz ground rice
about 2 tablespoons milk

1 Grease and line a 500 g/1 lb loaf tin with greaseproof paper and preheat the oven to 180°C/350°F/Gas Mark 4.

2 Cream together the butter and sugar until light and creamy. Then stir in the eggs. Fold in the flour and the ground rice. Add just enough milk to produce a soft consistency.

3 When the mixture is well mixed, transfer it to the prepared loaf tin and bake in the preheated oven for 45 minutes–1 hour, until cooked.

4 Turn out on to a cooling rack and allow to cool.

Christine Hill
Cleadon, Tyne and Wear

Preparation Time	20 minutes
Cooking Time	45 minutes–1 hour
Oven Temperature	180°C/350°F/Gas Mark 4

🧁 *Reader's Tip*

You can add lemon essence instead of milk. This is available in little bottles from grocers and supermarkets. If you don't have any to hand, add a few drops of lemon juice instead.

Polish Cake

125 g/4 oz margarine
1 tablespoon golden syrup
2 tablespoons drinking chocolate
175 g/6 oz plain cooking chocolate

BASE
250 g/8 oz digestive biscuits
25 g/1 oz margarine or butter, melted

1 Grease a 20 cm/8 inch round cake tin and line with clingfilm so that it comes up and over the sides.

2 Put the margarine, golden syrup and drinking chocolate in a pan and leave over low heat until all the ingredients are melted.

3 Now make the base. Crush the digestive biscuits and mix with the melted margarine or butter.

4 Place the biscuit mixture in the bottom of the cake tin, and pour the prepared syrup mixture on top.

5 Melt the cooking chocolate in a bowl over hot water. Pour the melted chocolate over the cake and place in the refrigerator until set.

Marion Wilson
Framfield, Sussex

Preparation Time	15 minutes
🧁 *Reader's Tip*	An easy way to crush digestive biscuits without making a dreadful mess is to place them in a polythene bag and then press a rolling pin over the top until all the biscuits are well broken up.

Moist Lemon Cake

125 g/4 oz soft margarine or butter
175 g/6 oz caster sugar
175 g/6 oz self-raising flour
1 teaspoon baking powder
2 large eggs
grated rind of 1 large or 2 small lemons
65 ml/2½ fl oz milk

LEMON SYRUP
3 tablespoons granulated sugar
juice of the lemon, or lemons, used to make the cake

1 Grease and line a 1 kg/2 lb loaf tin. Preheat the oven to 180°C/350°F/Gas Mark 4.

2 Place all the cake ingredients in a food processor and blend until really smooth and quite runny.

3 Pour the cake mixture into the prepared loaf tin and bake in the preheated oven for 45–50 minutes.

4 Meanwhile, make the lemon syrup. Dissolve the sugar in the lemon juice.

5 When the cooking time of the cake is up, test that the cake is done by pushing a metal skewer into the centre – if it comes out clean, it's done.

6 While the cake is still in the tin, place it on a cooling rack. Prick the cake all over with the skewer and spoon the lemon syrup all over the cake until you have used all the syrup. It will go everywhere, but do not worry – it will set when it is cold. Leave the cake in the tin until it is quite cold.

Pam Daniels
Norwich, Norfolk

'*This cake is without question my favourite. It won the Daily Telegraph prize for being the best foolproof cake.*'

Preparation Time	20 minutes
Cooking Time	45–50 minutes
Oven Temperature	180°C/350°F/Gas Mark 4

Reader's Tip

Use free-range eggs for your cakes – they are much better.

Coffee and Walnut Cake

125 g/4 oz self-raising flour
1 teaspoon baking powder
125 g/4 oz soft brown sugar
125 g/4 oz soft margarine
1 teaspoon coffee essence
2 eggs
25 g/1 oz chopped walnuts

COFFEE FROSTING
200 g/7 oz icing sugar
40 g/1½ oz butter
2 tablespoons water
25 g/1 oz caster sugar
2 teaspoons coffee essence

1 Grease and line two 18 cm/7 inch cake tins with greaseproof paper. Preheat the oven to 180°C/350°F/ Gas Mark 4.

2 Sift the flour and baking powder into a mixing bowl. Add the sugar, margarine, coffee essence, eggs and walnuts. Using a wooden spoon, mix to blend the ingredients and then beat well for 1 minute to obtain a smooth cake batter.

3 Divide the mixture between the prepared cake tins and spread level. Place in the centre of the preheated oven and bake for 25 minutes. Allow to cool in the tin for 2 minutes, then turn out and leave to cool completely.

4 Meanwhile, make the coffee frosting. Sift the icing sugar into a mixing bowl. Measure the butter, water, sugar and coffee essence into a saucepan and stir over a low heat until the butter has melted and the sugar dissolved.

5 Bring to the boil and pour at once into the sifted ingredients in the mixing bowl. Beat to a smooth glossy icing. Set aside until quite cold, then beat again to make a soft, gooey fudge icing.

6 Sandwich the cake layers with half of the coffee frosting. Spoon the remainder on top. Spread level and then rough up the icing with the tip of a knife to obtain a decorative finish.

Valerie Dunne
Manchester

'Coffee and walnuts marry well. Children might think they're "yucky", though, so don't risk it if you want to win the heart of a five-year-old.'

Preparation Time	30 minutes
Cooking Time	25 minutes
Oven Temperature	180°C/350°F/Gas Mark 4

Reader's Tip

This scrummy fudge frosting keeps well in the freezer.

117

Orange Gingerbread

75 g/3 oz butter
3 tablespoons golden syrup
75 g/3 oz soft brown sugar
175 g/6 oz self-raising flour
1 teaspoon mixed spice
1 teaspoon bicarbonate of soda
1½ teaspoons ground ginger
grated rind of 1 orange
1 egg
1 tablespoon orange juice
150 ml/¼ pint water

ORANGE ICING
175 g/6 oz icing sugar
1½ tablespoons orange juice

1 Grease and line an 18 cm/7 inch cake tin, 5 cm/2 inches deep. Preheat the oven to 160°C/325°F/Gas Mark 3.

2 Melt the butter, syrup and sugar over a low heat in a saucepan.

3 Sieve all the dry ingredients and beat in the butter mixture, orange rind and egg.

4 Boil the orange juice and water in the same pan and beat into the cake mixture.

5 Transfer the cake mixture into the prepared cake tin and bake in the preheated oven for 1¼–1½ hours. After 45 minutes, cover the top of the cake with two layers of non-stick baking parchment, with a round hold cut in the middle.

6 When the cake is cooked, allow it to cool in the tin.

7 To make the icing, sieve the icing sugar into a mixing bowl and gradually mix in the orange juice. Pour the icing on top of the cake.

J. K.
Pershore, Worcestershire

'The addition of orange rind and juice give this gingerbread a sharper taste.'

Preparation Time	30 minutes
Cooking Time	1¼–1½ hours
Oven Temperature	160°C/325°F/Gas Mark 3

Reader's Tip

Use the same quantity of black treacle instead of the golden syrup for a stronger, richer flavour.

Fruit Crusted Cider Cake

50 ml/2 fl oz golden syrup
150 g/5 oz butter or hard margarine
375 g/12 oz cooking apples, peeled, cored and finely chopped
50 g/2 oz mincemeat
50 g/2 oz cornflakes, crushed
125/4 oz caster sugar
2 eggs, beaten
125 g/4 oz self-raising flour, sifted
50 ml/2 fl oz dry cider

1 Grease and line a 35.5 × 11.5 cm/14 × 4½ inch shallow rectangular tart frame with aluminium foil. Grease the foil. Preheat the oven to 160°C/325°F/Gas Mark 3.

2 Put the syrup in a pan with 25 g/1 oz of the butter or margarine, and melt.

3 Add the apples, mincemeat and cornflakes. Stir together and set aside.

4 Put the remaining butter and the sugar in a mixing bowl and beat together until pale and fluffy. Gradually beat in the eggs.

5 Fold the flour into the mixture. Pour in the cider and mix in well.

6 Turn the mixture into the prepared frame and level the surface. Spread the apple mixture evenly over it.

7 Bake in the preheated oven for 45–50 minutes, or until firm to the touch.

8 Cool in the metal frame for 1 hour, then cut into bars for serving.

Gloria Cann
White Waltham

'*Apples, cider, mincemeat and cornflakes — the perfect ingredients to make a tasty cake.*'

Preparation Time	30 minutes
Cooking Time	45–50 minutes
Oven Temperature	160°C/325°F/Gas Mark 3

Reader's Tip

Bramleys are the best apples to use for this deliciously succulent cake. The cornflakes add an interesting variation in texture.

Sherry Biscuit Log

150 ml/¼ pint double cream
sherry, to taste
1 packet chocolate chip biscuits
1 chocolate flake

1 Whip the cream until stiff.

2 Pour the sherry into a small bowl. Take a biscuit and soak it in the sherry for about 10 seconds.

3 Soak the next biscuit and sandwich it to the previous one with whipped cream. Repeat the procedure until you have a log of cream-sandwiched biscuits on a large serving plate.

4 Use the remaining cream to cover the log completely. Crumble the flake over the log.

5 Chill in the refrigerator until ready to serve.

Geoff Skrone
Upavon, Wiltshire

Preparation Time	15 minutes

Reader's Tip

This recipe requires very little preparation and is proof that it is perfectly acceptable to construct something delicious from packets of biscuits and chocolate.

Ginger Biscuit Cake

300 ml/½ pint double cream
2 or 3 pieces stem ginger, finely chopped, plus
2 tablespoons of the syrup
24 ginger nuts

1 Whisk the cream until stiff.

2 Add the stem ginger and syrup.

3 Sandwich the biscuits together with ginger-flavoured cream and arrange in three columns of eight biscuits each on a large sheet of aluminium foil. Cover the biscuits with the remaining cream, then wrap up in foil and freeze.

4 Finally, remove from the freezer about 15 minutes before serving.

Lindy Moffatt
Hadlow Down, Sussex

Preparation Time	10 minutes

Reader's Tip

This cake makes a delicious pudding. An alternative to the use of stem ginger is to flavour the cream with crushed chocolate chip biscuits and coffee. Another idea is to melt some plain chocolate and drizzle this over the assembled cake.

Barbara's Brown Coffee Cake

300 g/10 oz soft light brown sugar
300 g/10 oz strong white flour
250 g/8 oz butter or margarine
1 teaspoon baking powder
1 teaspoon cinnamon
250 ml/8 fl oz buttermilk
1 teaspoon baking soda
1 egg
1 teaspoon vanilla essence
1 teaspoon instant coffee
50 g/2 oz pecan nuts

1 Grease a large flat rectanglar cake tin, 20 × 30 cm (8 × 12 inches). Preheat the oven to 190°C/375°F/Gas Mark 5.

2 Put the sugar, flour, butter or margarine, baking powder and cinnamon in a mixing bowl and mix together. Set aside about 325 g/11 oz of this mixture to top the cake.

3 Add the buttermilk, baking soda, egg, vanilla essence and instant coffee, and mix well. If the mixture curdles, just add a little more flour.

4 Pour the cake mixture into the prepared cake tin, and sprinkle on the reserved topping. Scatter the pecan nuts on top.

5 Bake in the preheated oven for 35–40 minutes.

Elisabeth Wengersky
South Hampstead, London

'*Eat this cake with freshly-brewed coffee for best results.*'

Preparation Time	15 minutes
Cooking Time	35–40 minutes
Oven Temperature	190°C/375°F/Gas Mark 5

Reader's Tip

In the absence of buttermilk, you can always use ordinary milk.

Linzer Torte

200 g/7 oz strong white flour
1 teaspoon baking powder
125 g/4 oz slightly salted butter, chilled
125 g/4 oz freshly ground fresh hazelnuts or almonds
125 g/4 oz caster sugar
15 g/½ oz vanilla sugar
2 drops bitter almond oil
¼ teaspoon ground cloves
1½ teaspoons ground cinnamon
1 egg white
½ egg yolk

FILLING
250 g/8 oz tangy-flavoured jam, such as raspberry,
redcurrant or morello cherry

TOPPING
½ egg yolk
1 teaspoon milk

1 Grease and line a round 26 cm/10½ inch spring-release cake tin. Preheat the oven to180°C/350°F/ Gas Mark 4.

2 Sieve the flour and baking powder on to a clean work surface, making a large well in the middle.

3 Coarsely grate the chilled butter all over the flour and sprinkle on the ground nuts, then put the caster sugar, vanilla sugar, almond oil, ground cloves, cinnamon, egg white and the half egg yolk into the well.

4 With your hands, work the dough together, first mixing the ingredients in the middle together and then gradually adding the flour. If the dough will not stick together, add a little water to bring it together.

5   When the dough is in one big ball, cut it in half and shape the 2 halves into balls. Put in a bowl or wrap them in clingfilm, and chill them in the fridge for at least 30 minutes for the pastry to rest. If your dough is quite soft, pop it in the freezer for 20 minutes so that it hardens up enough to roll out more easily.

6   Roll out one of the balls so that it covers the base only of your greased and lined tin. Line the tin, and go round the edges, pressing upwards a little. If the pastry is too soft and falls apart when you try to line the tin, you can take little bits of the pastry and press them into the tin with the back of a spoon until you have covered the base.

7   Spread the jam on to the base, leaving a 1 cm/$\frac{1}{2}$ inch border all around.

8   Roll out the remaining ball of pastry to the same size as the first one, and cut out enough strips to make a lattice pattern on top of the torte. If they are too long, don't worry – you can trim them up.

9   Seal the edges by pressing round the edges with a fork. Mix together the egg yolk and milk, and brush the top with this mixture. Bake in the preheated oven for 25–30 minutes.

Elisabeth Wengersky
South Hampstead, London

Preparation Time	20 minutes
Cooking Time	25–30 minutes
Oven Temperature	180°C/350°F/Gas Mark 4

⊙ *Reader's Tip*

This is a traditional Austrian tart. The butter needs to be chilled, or even frozen, so that it can be grated easily. It is important not to overcook the tart, so watch it carefully during the cooking process.

Elisabeth's Bottomless Cheesecake

a little butter, for greasing
500 g/1 lb curd cheese or fromage frais
150 ml/¼ pint soured cream
3 medium eggs, separated
grated rind of ½ lemon, plus a few drops lemon juice
50 g/2 oz currants or raisins (optional)
1 teaspoon cornflour or custard powder
½ teaspoon salt
3 heaped tablespoons sugar
15 g/¼ oz vanilla sugar
strawberries or kiwi fruit, sliced, to decorate

1 Lightly grease a 23 cm/9 inch flan dish using a little butter. Preheat the oven to 120°C/250°F/Gas Mark ½.

2 Put the curd cheese or fromage frais, soured cream, egg yolks, lemon rind and juice, currants or raisins, cornflour or custard powder, salt and 2 tablespoons of the sugar in a mixing bowl.

3 Beat the egg whites and, when they begin to stiffen, gently add the remaining sugar and the vanilla sugar.

4 Gently fold the egg whites into the cheese mixture using a metal spoon.

5 Pour into the prepared flan dish and bake in the pre-heated oven for about 1–1½ hours or until set.

6 Allow to cool and decorate with sliced strawberries or kiwi fruit.

Elisabeth Wengersky
South Hampstead, London

'This is the very best cheesecake
I have ever eaten.'

Preparation Time	20 minutes
Cooking Time	1–1½ hours
Oven Temperature	120°C/250°F/Gas Mark ½

Reader's Tip

Make this in the dish in which you wish to serve it, as it does not transfer easily. It is easy to make your own vanilla sugar. Put a vanilla pod in an airtight jar of caster sugar, and leave until required. The longer you leave it, the stronger the vanilla flavour. If you decide not to use the soured cream, perhaps because you're watching your figure, you should use only 2 eggs.

Acknowledgements

This book could not have been written without the help of many readers of *The Daily Telegraph, including:*

Muriel Allan, Lindsey Appleby, Rosie Ashe, Nan Ashman, Mrs. N. Ashworth, M. Atkinson, Heather Baker, Sheila Batten, Vera Beba, Daphne Blake, Moira Bourke, Michael Box, Pat Brown, Gloria Cann, Judy Cairns, Mrs. E. Clayton, Helen Cleave, M. Combourcha, Rosemary Cowan, Pam Daniels, Janet Dayer-Smith, Anne Dean, Eileen and Jenny, Sarah Donald, Valerie Dunne, Mary Dyson, Elizabeth, Emma Gardner, Gillian and Yvonne, Pauline Fairweather, Delia Gaze, Mary Gillies, Margaret Green, Jo Haines, Dorothy Harcourt, Jenny Heughan, Christine Hill, Norah Hinde, Griselda Hobson, Tony Hogger, Vera Hopwood, Sue Horsham, Jean Hurley, Sarah Innes, Barbara Jackson, Ivy Jarvis, Helen Kaczmarczuk, Cecilia J. Kee, Mrs. J.T. Kenner, J. K., Betty Jones, Daphne King-Brewster, Liz Kirkwood, Michael Lane, Anne Larpent, Diane Lawton, Joy Macdonald, Angela Master, Ann Meddings, Anne Mocatta, Lindy Moffatt, Mrs. J.V. Moss, Helen Orchard, Phillip D. Pearson, Rachel Perry, E. Ridout, Geoff Skrone, Karin Smith, Rev. Raymond Smith, Barbara Steele, Pamela Stevens, Gwen Stevenson, Patricia J. Stockham, Edna Terry, Susan Tomkins, Miss J.C. Turner, Elisabeth Wengersky, Mrs. M. West, Doreen Williamson, Marion Wilson, Jill M. White, Pam Whitwam and John Wright.

Every effort has been made by the Publishers and *The Daily Telegraph* to contact each individual contributor. If any recipe has appeared without proper acknowledgement, the Publishers and *The Daily Telegraph* apologise unreservedly. Please address any queries to the editor, c/o the Publishers.

Index